Mercy

A Restorative Philosophy

David J Cornwell

With a Foreword by Tapio Lappi-Seppälä

WATERSIDE PRESS

Mercy: A Restorative Philosophy
David J Cornwell

ISBN 978-1-909976-01-6 (Paperback)
ISBN 978-1-908162-77-9 (Epub ebook)
ISBN 978-1-908162-78-6 (Adobe ebook)

Main UK distributor Gardners Books, 1 Whittle Drive, Eastbourne, East Sussex, BN23 6QH. Tel: +44 (0)1323 521777; sales@gardners.com; www.gardners.com

North American distribution Ingram Book Company, One Ingram Blvd, La Vergne, TN 37086, USA. Tel: (+1) 615 793 5000; inquiry@ingramcontent.com

Cataloguing-In-Publication Data A catalogue record for this book can be obtained from the British Library.

Printed by Lightning Source.

e-book *Mercy* is available as an ebook and also to subscribers of Myilibrary, Dawsonera, ebrary, and Ebscohost.

Published 2014 by
Waterside Press
Sherfield Gables
Sherfield-on-Loddon
Hook, Hampshire
United Kingdom RG27 0JG

Telephone +44(0)1256 882250
E-mail enquiries@watersidepress.co.uk
Online catalogue WatersidePress.co.uk

Contents

This book is most respectfully dedicated to the Memory of

NELSON ROLIHLAHLA MANDELA

18 July 1918 to 5 December 2013
Lawyer, Human Rights Activist, Prisoner, Statesman,
Nobel Peace Laureate, First Democratically-elected President
of the Republic of South Africa 1994 to 1999.

An exemplar of courage, dignity, humility and forgiveness.
Loved by his nation: Mourned by the civilised world.

Acknowledgements

My grateful thanks are extended to all of those who have provided encouragement and support in the completion of this book, and in particular to my friend and colleague Professor John Blad of Erasmus University, Rotterdam, The Netherlands, who has insisted from its inception that it should be pursued to a conclusion.

I am also indebted, as ever, to Bryan Gibson and the staff at Waterside Press who have transformed the manuscript into its finished and indexed state with all their customary skill and attention to detail.

And finally, my sincere thanks to Dr Tapio Lappi-Seppälä, Director General of the National Research Institute of Legal Policy in Helsinki, Finland, for making the time within a very demanding work schedule to provide the Foreword to this work which is greatly appreciated and so clearly expressed.

David J Cornwell
Conderton
Gloucestershire
United Kingdom

May 2014

About the Author

Dr David J Cornwell is a consultant criminologist, former prison governor and tutor at HM Prison Service College, Wakefield. He has wide experience as a practitioner of custodial corrections in the public and private sectors in the UK and at Bloemfontein in the Republic of South Africa. He is the author of a trilogy of books on restorative justice: *Criminal Punishment and Restorative Justice* (2006), *Doing Justice Better* (2007) and *The Penal Crisis and the Clapham Omnibus* (2009), also of numerous journal articles and conference papers. With John Blad and Martin Wright he is the editor of *Civilising Criminal Justice* (2013). David Cornwell has undertaken consultancy assignments under the auspices of the Council of Europe in Poland (Themis Plan) and visited prisons in a number of European countries.

The author of the Foreword

Dr Tapio Lappi-Seppälä is the Director General of the National Research Institute of Legal Policy in Helsinki, Finland.

Foreword

Tapio Lappi-Seppälä[1]

This book is about doing criminal justice in a more humane and purposeful manner. It is a book that offers a new principled justification for restorative justice by linking it with another widely acknowledged concept and practice — that is of mercy.

The book challenges traditional deterrent and retributive penal philosophies, as well as the social and legal practices that have been conducted from these starting points. It grew, in the author's own words, from 'professional dissatisfaction with explanations of punishment and criminal justice theory and practice', and by 'acute awareness that in Britain in particular over the past decades criminal justice has become increasingly merciless towards offenders, while at the same time almost studiously avoiding affording victims of crime the status and empowerment that they evidently deserve'. These practices include over-reliance upon imprisonment; a phenomenon in Europe most visible in Britain. They include also the expansion of new and intrusive forms social control carried on outside traditional criminal justice, such as the widely used anti-social behaviour orders (ASBOs) in the UK.

Restorative justice, as formulated in the first writings in the late-1970s, was offered as an alternative to official criminal justice. This it never really became. Victims' rights did penetrate into high profile political speeches and even programmes, but far too often in the form of increased penalties and as a part of populist penal policy, not as truly reparative or restorative practices. This is one of the failures of restorative justice that David Cornwell's book seeks to correct.

Despite its short format, the book follows a highly ambitious programme. This is basically a book about the justification, aims and effects of criminal

1. Director General, National Research Institute of Legal Policy, Helsinki, Finland.

punishment. But it is also a philosophical treatise about the rarely discussed concept of mercy; a book about victim's rights; and a reform programme for the reorganizing of the criminal justice process. A reasoned discussion of all this calls for knowledge and understanding not only on the philosophy of punishment, but of criminological theories, existing social practices, and of empirical evidence on the effects of crime control. David Cornwell is able to bring all this to the table in an exciting and fresh manner.

Books and presentations on restorative justice are known for being filled with empathy and good intentions. This one incorporates also strict analyses and empirical evidence. The author's innovative idea of linking restorative justice with mercy raises the discussion of the justification of restorative justice to a more fundamental and principled level. The practical aim — formulating a criminal justice system that is less damaging, more purposeful, more humane, and does better justice for all parties — cannot be contested. And as such, this is a book for everyone concerned about the unfortunate state of our existing penal practices.

June 2014

Introduction

The reasons for this book are somewhat complicated, and yet if no explanation is offered or attempted, the work will have served no purpose. For almost 30 years I have written articles, papers, presentations and books focusing predominantly upon criminal punishment and, more recently, about restorative justice. Throughout this period of my life and also as a practitioner within prisons, both publicly and privately managed, in England and Wales and subsequently in South Africa, and as one with an enduring research interest in criminology, I, like so many of my colleagues, developed an increasing sense of professional frustration.

Having now, in 'semi- retirement', had the time to analyse this situation, I have come to the belief that throughout this period and its experiences, I had been plagued with a sense that since the 1960s and into this millennium there had existed an essential but missing ingredient within the criminal justice of the Anglo-Saxon tradition that made it increasingly 'unfit for purpose'. For while it is a relatively straightforward matter to detect the many reasons why criminal justice has 'stagnated' and largely failed in its essential purpose of crime reduction, particularly in relation to recidivism, it is altogether more difficult to discern why this failure has endured so persistently, and therefore what this 'missing ingredient' is both in theory and in practice.

One of the most profound and useful books in my criminological library, and a source to which I have frequently returned over the years, is H B Acton's *The Philosophy of Punishment: A Collection of Papers* published in 1979. It featured articles by some of the foremost philosophical thinkers of the post-World War Two era on aspects of crime and punishment, and these authors drew extensively on the work of others of equal stature in their arguments. Yet the final article in this compendium of learned papers was that by Alwynne Smart simply entitled 'Mercy' which had previously appeared in *Philosophy* in the October of the preceding year (Smart, 1978 and 1979: 212-228).

Now, Alwynne Smart's chapter seemed somehow to be one in an entirely different context from those preceding it, and one which also appeared to make a number of apparently self-evident suggestions about mitigation within the administration of punishment which, at first sight, seemed rather ordinary. Why, then, should it have been subsequently so important? I now believe that because it seemingly confused the notion of mercy with that of mitigation and *vice versa*, it caused me to consider why this might be a pivotal issue for criminal justice to resolve.

With the increasing growth of interest in restorative justice that has developed over the years since the decline of the 'justice model' conceived originally in the mid-1970s in the wake of the demise of the rehabilitative ethic, but progressively abandoned in the 1990s in favour of a return to retributive 'law and order' justice, there has arisen a consciousness of the fact that victims of crime have been considerably neglected and denied an appropriate status within criminal justice at both a conceptual and an operational level. This important deficiency has profound consequences for criminal justice administration if it is to be resolved as it most surely should be, but what has it to do with mercy?

The answer to this question is the essence of what this book is about. For reasons which will be traced back to the earliest practices of criminal justice across the world, and within many different cultural settings, it seems to me that proper recognition of victims and their status and the exercise of mercy are inextricably linked in the search for ways of making contemporary criminal justice 'fit for purpose'. It is towards this single end that this somewhat unusual and challenging book has been written.

Here it needs to be stated that this work might have been approached from a theological perspective invoking the early writings of Saint Thomas Aquinas in *Summa Theologiae* as to the 'affective' and the 'effective' motivations of the giver,[1] or from those of Saint Anselm on the nature of divine justice and mercy in *Proslogion*,[2] but neither would have provided the practical approach needed for this endeavour. It remains, at its core, a

1. For such an account of mercy see: R Stackpole (undated), 'Saint Thomas Aquinas on the Virtue of Mercy', from *Summa Theologiae* (ST II-II.30.1), available at: http://www.thedivinemercy.org/library/article.php
2. And here see: G Sadler (2006), 'Mercy and Justice in Saint Anselm's *Proslogion*', in *American Catholic Philosophical Quarterly*, Vol.80, No.1, pp.41-61 and: http://www.academia.edu/421015/mercy_and_justice_in_Saint_Anselm_Prologion.

'practitioner-focused' book, though drawing where necessary from the sometimes conflicting debates of moral and legal philosophy where these may be seen to be helpful to its purpose.

About this Book

I trust that the reader of this book will find that there is a coherent and logical structure within which its chapters are presented. It will be noted from *Chapter 1* that its 'point of departure' is somewhat uncertain, and the reason for this is also of importance. Dictionaries differ marginally in definitional expression of many of the terms we shall encounter. A 'philosophy' is generally regarded as 'a rational investigation of being, knowledge and right conduct, and the critical study of the basic principles and concepts of a discipline'.[3] This work therefore sets out to establish a restorative philosophy of mercy from a basis of principles and concepts that will become evident as it unfolds.

It is also the case that the present state of criminal justice in England and Wales, and in certain other democracies worldwide, has arrived at a curiously cyclical situation of 'stagnation' for a number of reasons. Supposed public 'fear of crime' that is largely media-inspired engenders equally supposed punitive public attitudes towards offenders. These, in turn, foster a retributive rhetoric among electorally sensitive politicians, concerned to be seen as 'tough on crime'. This situation leads to the enactment of increasingly draconian sentencing legislation which escalates prison populations, while at the same time preventing, or at least discouraging, exploration and implementation of alternative crime reduction strategies. Prisons, unable to serve the purposes for which they should be used due to the pressure of 'numbers', cannot hope to reduce offending behaviour, thus increasing the risk of recidivism. Offenders released from prisons and subsequently re-offending to an entirely unacceptable extent complete the cycle by increasing the potential for public anxiety.

The situation, stated thus briefly, raises the question of where to break into this cycle of despair to remedy the stagnation, and the wider question of whether the concept of mercy might, or could, assist in such an endeavour.

3. Here the definition in *Collins Dictionary of the English Language*, P Hanks (ed.), 1979 edition has been used, though that in the *Oxford English Dictionary* is in all senses similar.

It also begs the question of why the stagnation occurred in the first place, and these issues, among a number of others, provide the focus of the subsequent discussion within this work.

Some readers of this book may be surprised to note from its *Bibliography* the extent of scholarly writing and commentary that the concept of mercy has attracted over the years since the first publication of Alwynne Smart's article in 1968. The theological debate over mercy mentioned previously, and the Essay 'On Mercy' written by Seneca to the Emperor Nero *circa* 30AD and cited in *Chapter 1* are, of course, of considerably more ancient origin.

The Table of Contents that preceded this Introduction indicates the scope of each chapter. It is hoped that this has obviated the need for a more specific chapter-by-chapter description of the nature of the work at this stage. It remains a fact, however, that this book is as much about the concept of mercy as it is about that of restorative justice, and the potential for linkage between these two approaches for 'doing justice better'. Whether, or not, it achieves that purpose must now be left for the reader to decide.

CHAPTER ONE

An Uncertain Point of Departure

The Context of this Book

Conceptions of mercy within the philosophical literature of criminal and civil justice have occupied the minds of scholars for more than two thousand years,[1] and continue to do so. Much of this literature lies within the fields of ethics and moral philosophy which have invested the notion of mercy with an opacity that defies certainty of definition in a contemporary context. Moreover, many of the definitions of mercy that appear within writings on its place within operational justice show a tendency to confuse it with considerations relating to mitigation. This is largely unhelpful.

Processes of justice administration have existed in different cultural forms since recorded history began, many of these having deeply rooted origins in the perceived needs of early societies for social cohesion and the deprecation of wrongs and harms. In many of these societies of former times, the requirement for social harmony was of greater importance than the retributive punishment of offenders—particularly in instances in which wrongdoers were remorseful and willing to make apology and reparation to those offended against. The legacy of this more tolerant approach to crime persists in the indigenous populations of Africa, North America, Australasia, New Zealand, and some of the nations of the Middle-East, but has been widely disregarded in the countries of contemporary Western Europe.

The Middle-Ages in Western Europe—Justice in Transition

The emergence of centralised nation states during the later Middle-Ages in Europe effectively removed the administration of justice from the local level to that of national government, largely as a means of revenue generation

1. Certainly since the writings of Lucius Seneca *circa* 30 AD in a 'Moral Essay "On Mercy"' written to the Emperor Nero—see *Moral Essays*, II.ii.2-iv, 1-4, [Tr. J W Basore], The Loeb Classical Library, London: Heinemann.

through fines paid to sovereign treasuries rather than as compensation to victims of crime (Holdsworth, 1956:358; Jeudwine, 1917:155-6; Pollock and Maitland, 1898: 47; Gavrielides, 2011:9). This important transition, evident in England during the reign of King Henry II and also elsewhere in Western Europe, had two significant outcomes: the emergence of state controlled criminal justice and the demise of the victim as a primary stakeholder within the processes of justice (Geis, 1977: *passim*; Umbreit *et al.*, 2005:254-5).

The shift of emphasis within criminal and civil justice noted here had a further and enduring effect which to a considerable extent remains evident within contemporary responses to offending and offenders—particularly in Britain and in other countries that retain the Anglo-Saxon traditions of justice administration. It replaced the dominant notion of restitution with that of retribution for wrongdoing, justified on the premise that 'crime' was committed against the state rather than the victim. This 'centralisation' of state power in relation to criminal justice, although originally an initiative to establish monarchical authority over the traditional and localised structure of feudal fiefdoms and baronies, subsequently became reinforced by the emergence of powerful ecclesiastical elites concerned to assert and secure their powers—both spiritual and temporal—over populations.

Somewhat more importantly for the purposes of this work, however, the transition from restitutive (or reparative) to retributive justice that occurred progressively throughout the later Middle-Ages not only took away the right of victims to compensation and the expectation that wrongdoers should make reparation, but it also changed the concept of crime itself. As Pollock and Maitland have indicated: 'The wrong done to an individual extends beyond her own family; it is a wrong done to the community of which she is a member; and thus the wrongdoer may be regarded as a public enemy' (1898 *op. cit.*: *Ibid.*). The move towards state (or national) control of criminal justice ultimately resulted in crime being perceived as against the state rather than the individual whose right to restitution fell into desuetude. It also became the ultimate justification for retributive punishment.

It is also of interest to note that a somewhat parallel re-conception of crime became widespread during the same period in ecclesiastical dogma, and as Braithwaite has pointed out: 'It was the church that established prosecution as a central authority to assert its will and church heresy. The barbarism of the *Inquisition* was justified, because "crime" was committed not against the victim, but against the moral order of the church' (Braithwaite, 2002:7).

With the wisdom of hindsight, it became almost inevitable that the transition from communitarian/reparative to central/hierarchical government and justice would result in patterns of retributive punishment designed to impose the royal authority, and that of the landed nobility who owed a feudal duty to the crown in return for the granting of their estates. The latter, in particular, not only paid annual sums to the treasury to secure their entitlements, but were also responsible for ensuring that taxes were paid by the common people within their domains. King Henry I, the son of William the Conqueror, had issued a royal decree securing crown jurisdiction over a range of serious offences (treason, arson, robbery, murder, theft and other violent crimes) against the King's peace, many of which were punishable by death. In addition, common law juries were established during the reign of Henry II, with travelling Justices of Assize to preside over trials for capital (and some other) offences[2] (Jackson, 1940; Umbreit *et al., op. cit.*:255).

The early Middle-Ages witnessed a draconian approach towards the punishment of wrongdoing that extended for several centuries thereafter, and particularly within the lives of the lower social orders held in the feudal servitude and subsistence lifestyles of predominantly rural towns and villages throughout England.[3] Though a distinction had been developed between criminal and civil wrongs (or torts) within the justice system, such was relatively meaningless in the lives of the peasant classes whose daily existence and subsistence relied upon manual labour for which minimal wages were paid. Access to justice for those wronged became increasingly remote other

2. Among such other offences were included witchcraft, the poaching of royal game, theft of livestock, rape, the counterfeiting of coinage, heresy and vagrancy. Charges of witchcraft and heresy were normally tried in the ecclesiastical courts under the jurisdiction of bishops.
3. By way of example, the privilege of *infangthief* and *outfangthief* granted as standard practice by the crown to landowners after the Norman Conquest entitled local lords to execute summary justice on thieves and other criminals. The terms relate to those captured within the estates of the lord, or even beyond the estates having committed crime within them, to be returned to face justice meted out by the lord himself. The captor of the thief was given a choice between summarily executing him or her—the usual fate for the poor—or of ransoming him or her for a fine set according to his or her status. The privilege was both profitable and a means of maintaining discipline within estates and of enhancing the authority of its holder. For a further explanation see: Walter W Lewis (1987), *The Governance of Norman and Angevin England 1086-1272*, Stanford, ILL: Stanford University Press, p.45.

than by appeal to local lords whose writ ran unquestioned throughout the length and breadth of the country.

The progressive decline in the status of victims of crime evident from the Plantagenet era onwards[4] resulted in retributive justice becoming increasingly established as the principal justification within criminal punishment, enhanced by an intuitive belief in the efficacy of severity as a means of deterring potential offenders through the public spectacle of executions and other corporal measures such as flogging and physical mutilation.[5] It was not until the early 16th-century that Sir Thomas More (1478-1535) in his work *Utopia* published in 1515 argued the first reasoned plea for a return to the practice of offenders making restitution to their victims by working for the public to earn the means of doing so.[6]

More's plea for a less brutal and more purposeful use of criminal sanctions made little impact upon criminal justice policy-making for almost three centuries thereafter, and it was not until a succession of international prison congress meetings held between 1878 and 1900 promoted a return to restorative practices and restitution of victims that any serious interest was shown in doing so—at least in Britain. The members of these congress meetings did, however, pass a resolution urging their respective nation states to increase the rights of victims under the civil law (Gavrielides, 2011 *op. cit.*:12).

From the mid-1800s and onwards in Britain, and largely due to the insistent pressure from penal reformers such as John Howard, Jeremy Bentham, John Austin, and somewhat later Samuel Romilly and Elizabeth Fry, penal conditions were improved with the construction of numerous new prisons based on the design of penitentiaries pioneered in America. These prisons were placed under the control of the Directors of Convict Prisons approved by the Home Secretary, and subsequently of the Prison Commissioners established by the Prison Act 1877 (Walker, 1972 *op. cit.*:122-3).

Further progress towards more civilised justice and prison conditions

4. That is, from the reign of King Henry II, which began in 1154, until the death of King Richard III in 1485 in England.
5. For a graphic account of the various methods used in the physical and psychological infliction of punishments on criminal offenders from the 13th-century onwards in Britain and Europe, see Peter N Walker (1972), *Punishment: An Illustrated History*, Newton Abbot: David and Charles (Publishers) Limited.
6. T S More [1990](1515), *Utopia: New Haven*, London: Yale University Press.

was hampered by the two World Wars of the 20th-century (1914-1918) and (1939-1945) and the periods of international reconstruction that followed both conflicts. This stated, however, the central components of punishment philosophy (retribution and deterrence) remained largely unchallenged until the emergence of restorative justice in the 1970s with the work of Albert Eglash, Howard Zehr and subsequently many others (Eglash, 1975; Zehr, 1990, 2002; Zehr and Mika, 1998; Wright, 1996).[7]

For the purposes of this work, however, the brief history of penology outlined in the foregoing paragraphs suffices to indicate the central premise that will be developed in the chapters which follow. It is that when, during the Plantagenet era, the state 'stole' justice from its communities[8], the 'virtue' of mercy was effectively discarded in favour of retribution, and has never been reinstated. It will further be proposed that mercy has an essential place within justice that only restorative justice is capable of enabling both in theory and in practice.

This much asserted, a careful review of the surprisingly extensive literature on mercy reveals that there has existed a considerable extent of debate and confusion as to what it consists in, and also as to what is supposed, often misleadingly, about it. On the one hand, much of the literature stemming from the academic disciplines of ethics and moral philosophy is at the least contentious to the point of confusion and even of disagreement. It does, however, provide an avenue of approach which cannot reasonably be discounted. On the other hand, if the potential for the reinstatement of mercy is to be given a practical purpose—as I shall propose that it deserves—then an altogether different approach becomes not only desirable, but also unavoidable—hence, the selection of the title of this chapter.

---

7. During the years immediately following World War Two and into the 1980s there was a period of considerable confusion within penology and criminology worldwide that focused on the 'treatment' and rehabilitation of offenders, but which was overtaken by the emergence of the 'justice model' of punishment with origins in the USA, and espousing proportionality in sentencing as a primary motivation. This model also fell into disfavour during the late-1980s and early-1990s with a return to more punitive penal policies in Britain and elsewhere in North America and Western Europe in particular.
8. Here see Nils Christie (1977), 'Conflicts as Property', *British Journal of Criminology*, 17(1), pp.1-15.

The Later 20th-Century: The Need for a Different Justice Paradigm

At much the same time as Albert Eglash (1977, *op. cit.*) was formulating his concept of restorative justice, Randy Barnett was also writing about restitution as a means of resolving what he perceived as a 'paradigm crisis' within criminal justice in which it had become urgently necessary to replace retributive punishment policies with a more constructive and socially useful use of sanctions based upon the restitution of victims of crime (Barnett, 1977:245). Eglash had identified three prevailing models of criminal punishment as being either in use or potentially available at the time: retributive, distributive and restorative. The first two, he maintained, focused exclusively on the criminal act, denied victim participation in the justice process, and required only passive participation by offenders. The third, however, placed emphasis on restoring the harmful effects of wrongdoing, and had the potential to involve actively all the parties in the criminal justice process. Restorative justice, he maintained, provided 'a deliberate opportunity for offender and victim to restore their relationship, along with a chance for the offender to come up with a means to repair the harm done to the victim'.

The urgency of the (then) perceived need for a 'paradigm shift' lay in a widespread dissatisfaction and confusion within many criminal justice systems worldwide over the demise of the rehabilitative ethic during the early-1970s, and the emergence of the 'justice model' of corrections in the United States of America as proposed initially by the American Friends Service Committee (1972), and subsequently developed by Andrew von Hirsch in a major work *Doing Justice* in 1976. History records that the 1970s and 1980s were also years of great turbulence and unrest in prisons in the USA and in Britain: riots and disorder became the means by which prisoners demonstrated their demands for improved conditions, less crowding, and an extension of their perceived 'rights'. The 'justice model' was predicated upon proportionality of punishment to crime, determinacy in sentencing, the limitation of judicial and administrative discretion, an end to disparity in sentencing, and the protection of 'rights' through due process (Hudson, 1987:38-48).

Moreover, as Barbara Hudson further noted, the initial appeal of the' justice model' lay in the fact that it appeared to offer all things to all people:

> To the liberal lawyers, it promised a restoration of the legitimacy and respect accorded the legal system by reducing the perceived irrationality and unfairness of a system that facilitated—and indeed logically depended upon—wide discretion and disparity in sentencing, with like offences receiving very unlike sentences (e.g. Frankel, 1973; Fogel, 1975; Wilkins, 1980); to the right-wing law-and-order lobby it appeared to guarantee 'swift and sure punishment', ending leniency and the softly, softly approach of giving criminals over into the hands of social workers rather than into the control of the prison system (e.g. Wilson, 1977; Morgan, 1978); to radical academics, social workers and campaigners against the excessive use of imprisonment, considering the offence meant that the huge volume of petty, routine offending would be punished by conditional discharges, fines, etc. and imprisonment would become reserved for only the most serious, most socially or physically dangerous of criminals, and that people would cease to be imprisoned because of judicial prejudice against the unemployed, members of ethnic minority groups, the young and already socially disadvantaged (e.g. American Friends Service Committee, 1972; Shur, 1973; Morris, 1978) (Hudson, 1987, *op. cit.*: 37–38).

In the event, the 'justice model' went into a swift decline during the mid-to-late-1980s due, in both Britain and America, to a return to right-wing politics and public disenchantment with penal systems that failed to reduce the volume of criminal offending, and in particular, re-offending by those released from custodial sentences. The resulting vacuum in penal policies was immediately filled by a return to retributive sentencing allied to uncritical belief that harsher punishment would deter both offenders and would-be offenders, and thereby reduce criminal activity.

The Penological Vacuum and the Naissance of Restorative Justice

It was against this back-drop that restorative justice struggled to establish a foothold in the early years following its initial elaboration by Eglash, Zehr, and other of its founding proponents, and continued to do so into the new millennium. It has also to be accepted that whatever its merits, restorative justice as originally conceived suffered from vulnerability to criticism in two important respects: the first that it was essentially a 'practitioner-led' initiative appealing to moral intuition and lacking a clearly elaborated, evidence-led, and universally adopted philosophical framework; and the second which stems from the first, that it was adapted and 'localised' by its adherents to meet the cultural needs of the many different societies worldwide in which it did gain early acceptance.

In all fairness, however, it is self-evidently obvious that it is difficult to establish an evidence-led philosophy in circumstances in which there exists a traditional reluctance to depart from politically-motivated retributive punishment agendas and enable reparative and restorative practices to be implemented and evaluated in a rigorous manner. Such is certainly the case in relation to relatively serious offending, since to do so can be claimed to carry an element of public risk, and politicians and their policy advisers are notoriously risk-averse. Thus however deeply-seated the existing paradigm crisis may be, the paradigm-shift that might resolve it will be viewed with considerable reservation and antipathy.

Since the early years of the present decade there have been signs that successive governments in England and Wales (and elsewhere) have noted the restorative justice agenda and have been prepared to explore its effectiveness at the margins of the criminal justice system, most particularly in the area of youth justice. Indeed, in November 2012 the Ministry of Justice published a document bearing the title *Restorative Justice Action Plan for the Criminal Justice System* (Ministry of Justice, 2012a). This particular document differs significantly from others published previously (e.g. Home Office, 2003a; 2003b; 2005a; 2005b; 2005c; and 2005d) in that it specifically focuses on the victim-offender relationship rather than the responsibilities of the various departments of state involved in the justice process (police, courts, probation and prison services, the youth justice sector, the prosecution service, etc.). Moreover, the Report of the Criminal Justice Joint Inspectorate (CJJI), *Facing up to Offending: Use of Restorative Justice in the Criminal Justice System*, published in September 2012 (Ministry of Justice, 2012b) highlighted a range of 'current limitations' and key issues that need to be addressed to achieve consistent implementation of restorative justice techniques. Summarily, these were:

- Low public awareness of RJ — especially among victims;
- Lack of clarity, often misunderstanding of what RJ is;

- Need to strengthen the 'statutory footing' of RJ in the criminal justice system—particularly with adults;
- Patchy understanding in criminal justice agencies of the role and outcomes of RJ;
- Patchy provision of RJ across the 'justice chain', i.e. out of court, in court, community sentencing and prisons;
- Access to RJ in both youth and adult sectors can be radically improved;
- Need for on-going monitoring and evaluation of RJ practices;
- Need to ensure that best practice is upheld and maintained;
- Lack of a government-based forum to discuss the future policy and operational direction.

In respect of the latter limitation, the Action Plan indicates that the government intends that the responsibility for overseeing its delivery will pass to a new Restorative Justice Implementation Board which will report regularly to ministers on the progress being made (Ministry of Justice, 2012a *op. cit.*:7).[9]

It would be fanciful to suggest that the path towards establishment of reparative and restorative justice as a central element of criminal (or civil) justice in an Anglo-Saxon context will be speedily implemented or free from objection from a range of potential sources. As became the experience in Finland during the later decades of the 20th-century, radical change in the administration of justice requires a wide social consensus of vested interests which at the least includes politicians, policy-makers, the judiciary, lawyers, prosecutors, academics, practitioners, police, the media and the general population (Lappi-Seppälä, 2013: 501-524; Joutsen *et al.*, 2001). It is, however, capable of achievement.

There is also no doubt that the penal systems of England and Wales and

9. The Restorative Justice Implementation Board should not be confused with the Restorative Justice Council which is a non-governmental body established in 1997 as the Restorative Justice Consortium and which gained charitable status under its new name in 2010. The council and the former consortium brought together a membership of practitioners, academics and others interested in promoting restorative justice in resolving conflict in public life in a wide range of situations beyond criminal justice—most notably in education, industrial relations and similar arenas.

of a number of other nations worldwide are presently in the grip of a 'paradigm crisis' which shows no sign of being resolved other than through radical systemic and philosophical change. A move towards genuine incorporation of reparative and restorative justice could provide the 'paradigm shift' that is necessary to fuel such reform, while providing a more reasoned and effective form of justice administration for the future, and at much lesser social and financial cost.

The title of this book focuses on the role of mercy in establishing a restorative philosophy for better justice. This means a return to the reparative justice of centuries past, pillaged by motivations of retribution and the denial of restitution to those most harmed by wrongdoing. In the chapter that follows, the argument for a re-definition of mercy within justice will be put forward in a restorative philosophical context, and as a means towards setting out the foundations for reformed justice delivery. In so doing, the claims of other approaches to the virtue of mercy will also be examined, and, where it seems necessary, the shortcomings of these approaches will be identified and explained.

CHAPTER TWO

The Need for Definition

The debate about the place of mercy within the philosophy and practice of criminal justice has intermittently penetrated the discourses of the past 50 years, particularly in the academic disciplines of moral and legal philosophy, criminology, and to a certain extent also of theology. That it continues to surface periodically only to re-submerge in an inconclusive morass of ethical disagreement is scarcely surprising. For everyone knows what mercy is, whether perceived as a virtuous necessity, an ameliorating intervention, or even as an act of forbearance or compassion. Yet however virtuous mercy may appear to be, it is also seen by some as having an intrusive or 'weak' quality that is not inevitably consistent with justice or moral 'rightness'.

Such an analysis propels us towards the awkward but inevitable question of how 'just' our processes of jurisprudence actually are, both in concept and in practice. The 'legality' of laws may be beyond question as enacted by parliaments, but in some instances the outcomes of their implementation are most certainly questionable.[1] It therefore seems appropriate to begin this chapter with a brief definitional examination of the meanings and characteristics ascribed to justice, equity, mitigation and mercy in turn, since each has an historical and an ethical significance for the processes of criminal punishment and sentencing.

Justice Defined

Dictionary definitions vary marginally, but there is a consensus that justice consists in the quality (or fact) of being just—or even righteous, of being

1. Such, for instance, as the provisions in the Criminal Justice Act 2003 in England and Wales for indeterminate or extended detention in the interests of public protection from serious violent and/or sexual offenders on the basis of predicted future dangerousness. At the end of March 2012 there were 6,017 prisoners serving indeterminate imprisonment for public protection (IPP) sentences, and of these, 3,506 were detained beyond their tariff expiry dates (Prison Reform Trust, 2012:5).

impartial and equitable, and of rendering to every person his or her due. Within ethics, justice is the moral principle that determines the fairness of actions, and within law it consists in its administration in terms of legal validity, and according to prescribed and accepted principles.

In the rather narrower context of penology, such a definition leads inevitably to consideration of desert about which there is much more to be discussed within this work, since it leads to pivotal and yet conflicting issues of principle that affect both the working and the outcomes of the processes of justice in practice.

The requirement that justice should be equitable also gives rise to debatable issues of interpretation as we shall see subsequently. Yet at this stage in the discussion it will already be evident that there is a sense in which justice and equity are inextricably linked, and are to a considerable extent interdependent.

This same definition of justice further implies that laws display a quality of 'goodness': such is to suggest that in a conceptual sense laws are universally applicable and work to the benefit of all those subject to their provisions and in the interest of common (or social) well-being. This, in turn, suggests that 'good' laws must transcend the narrow interests of political motivation in order to make justice impartial as between classes of persons whose duty it becomes to act in conformity with them.

Its Relationship with Equity

At first sight, equity seems to have a meaning similar to that of justice insofar as it includes the qualities of being impartial, fair and reasonable. Further, however, equity in a legal sense implies a system of jurisprudence founded on principles of natural justice and fairness, but yet displaying the means to correct or supplement the provisions of statute law by making it conform to its reason or spirit, and also apply to cases for which the law does not expressly provide.[2]

Equity, therefore, introduces an element of interpretive discretion in

2. Here it will be noted that those entrusted with the drafting of laws cannot reasonably be expected to devise provisions that meet every conceivable contingency, but rather express the intention of the law to provide for and meet the generality of cases falling within the forms of conduct that each law is designed to promote or forbid.

pursuit of fairness, allowing the spirit of the law to override its literal meaning in instances unusual or unforeseen. Thus equity includes the consideration of circumstances that reasonably necessitate or obligate leniency (Lauchs, 2005:2), and, by implication, of aggravation also.[3] Considerations of equity also suggest the further general principle of treating like cases in a like manner, though as will subsequently become clear, such a principle is a general one since in reality, apparently like cases are far from identical when circumstances of mitigation and aggravation are taken into account.

The Place of Mitigation

Mitigation has an important role to play *within* the legal process once a finding of guilt has been reached and issues of culpability (or blameworthiness) have to be considered in deciding upon appropriate sanctions in response to offence(s) committed. It brings to the formal attention of the court evidential reasons in two forms for imposing a penalty lesser in severity than might otherwise have been deemed to be deserved in relation to the seriousness of the offence(s) proven.

Offence mitigation raises matters related to the commission of the offence itself, while *offender* mitigation offers aspects of the background and any special circumstances of the offender that might enable the court to take a more lenient view of how and why the offence took place. As Gibson (2009) points out, 'a considerable body of law and precedents cover what can and cannot amount to mitigation in given circumstances, the extent to which it should have any effect, and what is expressly not mitigation' (Gibson, 2009:109).[4]

Pleas in mitigation of sentence in relation to the commission of offences may seek to indicate that these took place under some or another form of duress, or that the accused had no original intention of committing them, or was in some way provoked into doing so or acted in self-defence. Offender mitigation may focus on the personal circumstances of the accused and his/her background, the extent of any genuine remorse or contrition shown

3. In his interpretation of equity in this particular sense, Mark Lauchs (2005) did not refer to the matter of aggravation which I have added in the interest of clarity in subsequent discussion.
4. In this connection, however, it should be noted that mitigation cannot affect a mandatory sentence such as that of life imprisonment for murder.

towards the victim(s) of the offence(s), or the presence of medical or psychiatric conditions that had a direct bearing on his/her actions at the time of offence commission.

It should, however, be noted here that while mitigation may plead for leniency or parsimony in punishment, this is a matter entirely different from issues relating to the exercise of mercy to which we now turn attention.

The Characteristics of Mercy

Mercy is widely described and accepted as a 'virtue' of justice, even though its exercise lies *outside* or beyond the processes by which justice is administered. Strictly viewed, it can only be brought into operation once legal deliberations have been concluded, and it has clearly defined characteristics. Though definitions differ marginally, there exists a general consensus that mercy amounts to the exercise of forbearance or compassion by one person towards another in demanding less than the full extent of severity or recompense due to, or arising from, that other person's wrongful act(s) or omission(s).

The characteristics of mercy are that one person must have another within his power or care; that the person within this power has no prior claim to receive kindness, forbearance or compassion; that the severity of the recompense imposed was justly and lawfully due; and that forbearance and compassion were extended notwithstanding. As will become clear in subsequent discussion, such a definition raises a number of issues which have undoubtedly led to debate and controversy in relation to the exercise of mercy in both civil and criminal justice.

The first, and possibly the most important of these issues is that the severity of the recompense (or penalty) imposed was strictly deserved and proportionate to the harm occasioned. The second, and in the context of British justice also contentious, is that the person extending mercy must be a legitimate stakeholder within the justice process in order to be empowered to do so. A third, and philosophically complex issue of debate is the claim made by some that the exercise of mercy conflicts with the principle of treating like cases alike, and that it also runs counter to that of desert within the philosophy of punishment.

These potential or actual objections have to be treated with the seriousness that is evidently deserved, and I shall attempt to do this in a later part of this chapter. For the present, however, it must suffice to have proposed the foregoing definitions in order to enable discussion of a relatively recent and widely debated instance of the supposed exercise of mercy within criminal justice in the United Kingdom by way of illustration.

The Extraordinary Case of Abdelbaset Ali Mohmed al-Megrahi

On 21st December 1988, a Pan Am Flight 103 Jumbo Jet was blown up in mid-air over the town of Lockerbie in Scotland killing 270 people of whom 259 were passengers and crew, and 11 residents in the town. The flight was outbound from Frankfurt to New York carrying many American citizens and service personnel and their dependants returning to spend the Christmas and New Year holiday in the USA. Though the identity of the perpetrators of the atrocity remained uncertain for some time, suspicion eventually focused on the North African state of Libya which was known to give sanctuary and training to terrorist organizations and dissident groups throughout the Middle-East and Near-East.

The American Federal Bureau of Investigation (FBI) and the United Kingdom counter-terrorist authorities spent many months in attempting to identify those responsible for the bombing, and eventually, in November 1991, Abdelbaset al-Megrahi[5] and another co-accused Lamin Khalifah Fhimah were indicted by the US Attorney General and the Scottish Lord Advocate, and demands were made for their extradition to stand trial in Scotland. The demands were refused by the Libyan government. After further negotiations, Libya held the two suspects under house arrest in Tripoli, offering to detain them for trial in that country providing that all incriminating evidence against them was submitted for consideration.

The offer was unacceptable to both the USA and the UK, and a three-year period of *impasse* followed while sporadic negotiations continued and United Nations sanctions against Libya were imposed. Eventually, it was agreed that the two accused men would be extradited to stand trial in The Netherlands under Scottish law, and in April 1999, ten years after the bombing had taken place, the two were placed under arrest at Camp Zeist there to face the

5. Abdelbaset al-Megrahi was Head of Security for Libyan Arab Airlines, and Director of the Centre for Strategic Studies in Tripoli, Libya. He was also an alleged Libyan intelligence officer.

murder charges lodged against them. Their trial lasted some eight months starting on 5th May 1999, and on 31st January 2001 al-Megrahi was convicted of murder on 270 counts by the special Scottish High Court of Justiciary comprising three Scottish judges (and a fourth non-voting judge) sitting without a jury, and was sentenced to life imprisonment for a minimum period of 20 years. His co-accused (Lamin Fhimah) was found not guilty and acquitted, having provided alibi evidence of having been in Sweden at the time of the bombing. Al-Megrahi was imprisoned in Scotland, initially at Barlinnie Prison, and subsequently at Greenock.[6]

Both al-Magrahi and Fhimah had maintained their innocence during the trial, and in January 2001 al-Magrahi appealed against his conviction on the grounds that it was unsafe due to equivocal evidence provided by one key witness (Tony Giauci—a Maltese shopkeeper who had testified that he had sold al-Megrahi items of clothing later found in the remains of the suitcase bomb retrieved from the wreckage of the aircraft). His appeal was rejected on 14th March 2002 by a panel of five Scottish judges sitting once again at Camp Zeist. Further appeals and reviews followed between 2003 and 2007, the latest being heard by the Scottish Criminal Cases Review Commission (SCCRC) as an appeal against both conviction and sentence.[7]

Following the four year review conducted by the SCCRC and concluded in June 2007, the commission had uncovered evidence that a miscarriage of justice could have occurred, and granted al-Megrahi leave to appeal once again against his conviction. This appeal to the Court of Criminal Appeal was subsequently abandoned in August 2009 as there had arisen an impediment to the legal powers to release him to Libya under the terms of the Prisoner Transfer Scheme then in operation within the United Kingdom. Meanwhile, however, in August 2008 al-Megrahi had been diagnosed as

6. An excellent account of the circumstances surrounding the Lockerbie bombing, the trial of the accused al-Megrahi and Lamin Fhimah, and the subsequent series of appeal hearings against al-Megrahi's conviction may be found at http://en.wikipedia.org/wiki/Abdelbaset_al-Megrahi

7. In November 2003 al-Magrahi had appeared at the High Court in Glasgow before the three judges who had originally sentenced him, to be informed that due to the incorporation into Scottish law of the European Convention on Human Rights in 2001, his sentence would be one of 27 years before he could be considered for parole, backdated to April 1999 when he was extradited from Libya. The convention requires that all persons convicted and sentenced to life imprisonment must be informed of the 'tariff' period of their sentence—i.e. that necessary to meet the requirements of retribution and deterrence in relation to their offences.

suffering from advanced and terminal prostrate cancer, and had a limited time left to live—possibly a period of months.

On the 4th August 2009, the Justice Minister for Scotland (Kenneth MacAskill) visited Greenock Prison to hear al-Megrahi's request for a prisoner transfer to Libya, and al-Megrahi subsequently applied for his outstanding appeal against conviction to be discontinued. On 19th August 2009 it was announced that the minister had reached a decision on al-Megrahi's request, and on the following day MacAskill announced that al-Megrahi was to be released on compassionate grounds due to his terminal medical condition, and would be returned to Libya. Almost immediately following upon the announcement, al-Megrahi was escorted by Strathclyde Police to Glasgow Airport where he boarded a specially chartered Afriqyah Airways Airbus for Tripoli. He subsequently died on 20th May 2012 in Tripoli, aged 60 years.

Finally, by way of a footnote on this case, it has to be added that during the period of al-Megrahi's imprisonment in Scotland, there had arisen widespread local and international unease over his conviction. The Moderator of the General Assembly of the Church of Scotland (Iain Torrance) was among the first to call for his release or re-trial, followed by Nelson Mandela who in early 2003 asked for the intervention of the Western Christian Churches in what he described as a 'clear miscarriage of justice'. Tam Dayell, the former Labour MP for West Lothian concurred with such a view, as did the South of Scotland SNP MSP Christine Grahame. Even Dr Jim Swire, the spokesman for UK Families Flight 103 whose daughter Flora had been a victim at Lockerbie, became convinced that al-Megrahi had become the victim of a gross miscarriage of justice, and was innocent of the Lockerbie atrocity. The question remains: was justice done?

The Ensuing Debate—The Opinion of Professor Anthony Duff

The eventual release of Abdelbaset Ali al-Megrahi provoked a major political and philosophical debate not only within Scotland and the other parts of the United Kingdom and in America, but also on a worldwide basis. Fortunately for the purposes of this work, the issues involved may be seen to have been encapsulated in an exchange of articles in late-2009 between two highly respected and learned scholars in Scotland—Professors Anthony Duff[8] and Lindsay Farmer (Duff, 2009a and b; Farmer, 2009.[9]

In the opening article of the exchanges, Duff acknowledged that there were reasonable and respectable grounds for the decision to release al-Megrahi, and continuing doubts about his guilt and original conviction, but that the decision to release him was on balance wrong. He further conceded that the court sentenced al-Megrahi to life imprisonment as an appropriate sentence for the crime of which he had been convicted, and that the sentence was deserved and not disproportionately harsh. Moreover, if the sentence was a just one, it was one that justice not only permitted, but also required. And if it was required at the time it was imposed, the fact that al-Megrahi became terminally-ill could not make a difference to what he deserved and was required thereafter. Indeed, it would have been unjust for the court to have imposed a lesser sentence than that which he deserved.

Going somewhat further, Duff pointed out that the sentence was in part 'owed' to the victims of the crime to indicate that the harm they had suffered was viewed with appropriate seriousness, and to hold those responsible for it to proper account. It was also in part 'owed' to the 'political' or civic community whose collective values had been violated in a public sense, and that this should be taken seriously and responded to in a way that justice demands. Thus the courts and those who administer the criminal justice system have a duty to do what justice requires, and if, for whatever reason, they remit or lighten the punishment that justice demands, they fail in that duty.

In concluding his article, Duff drew attention to the fact that by imposing punishment it is intended that the wrongdoer should be obliged to focus upon his crime, the harm he had done to others, and consider how this might be 'put right' as a means to his eventual restoration to full civic status. The fact that al-Megrahi became terminally-ill did not, in Duff's view, change this obligation which was intended, through the duration of the sentence

8. Anthony Duff is a Professor of Philosophy at Stirling University, and has written extensively on the philosophy of criminal law and punishment. His particular work on communicative theory, *Punishment, Communication and Community*, (2000, Oxford University Press) addressed the problem of justifying punishment.

9. Lindsay Farmer is Professor of Law at Glasgow University Law School, and Editor in Chief of the journal *New Criminal Law Review*. Among his recent publications is a three volume collaboration on the criminal trial (with S Marshall, M Renzo and V Tadros) published by Oxford University Press in 2010, 2011 and 2013 respectively.

imposed upon him, to occupy his mind for a number of years. Thus it would have been appropriate and humane for him to be helped as far as possible to face his own death while doing so, or even to have been returned to a Libyan prison had that been feasible, but for a crime of that magnitude, the decision to release him 'was to allow a merciful impulse to override, rather than appropriately to temper, the demands of justice' (Duff, 2009a *op. cit.*: 4).

Professor Lindsay Farmer's Response to Duff

In his reply to Anthony Duff, Lindsay Farmer acknowledged the eloquence of Duff's article which, he noted, 'focused attention on central issues which any account of mercy must address', but found that he disagreed with Duff on two important issues. The first of these was that it was unjust not to impose a deserved sentence, and the second the specific conclusion that the decision of Kenneth MacAskill was on balance wrong because a merciful impulse overrode the demands of justice rather than tempering it.

Pointing out the historical legacy of mercy as a virtue exercised once the legal process had been exhausted, Farmer suggested that as the modern criminal justice system evolved, the power to exercise mercy 'was subtly transformed . . . while still exercised in the name of the sovereign, it ceased to be exercised by the sovereign directly. The power was delegated to ministers of the crown — formerly the Secretary of State for Scotland and now the Justice Minister — to be exercised on behalf of the crown. Crucially, however, in this process the power was legalised; it can only be exercised by the legally recognised person, according to established legal procedures. It remains in this sense an executive power beyond justice.'(Farmer, 2009 *op. cit.*1-2).

This modern legalisation of mercy, as Farmer maintained, leads to something of a paradox: in law the issue is whether the power to extend mercy has been properly used and the procedures correctly followed; and in politics the issue arises because the minister is answerable to Parliament for having decided appropriately that the case was one in which it was right to extend mercy. Moreover as he further suggested, if the exercise of mercy is beyond the law, it must also be beyond punishment or desert. In Duff's interpretation of the situation it would seem that the duty of the state in punishing offenders is not discharged until the full sentence has been served, and therefore the state cannot assume the two roles of doing justice and exercising mercy. Farmer believed this to be a fallacy for the reason indicated above, and for another that he then addressed.

Farmer further insisted that the exercise of mercy within criminal justice consisted not in questions of proportion or measures of desert, but in doing what is appropriate or right in the circumstances of each case, and in a humane and compassionate manner when there is an evident need to do so. Thus, mercy tempers the strict demands of justice, but remains external to it. It was in this particular respect that he found Duff's limited recognition of a place for mercy troubling.

There is, in our contemporary systems of justice, a clear distinction between the state's duty to punish offenders which is typically undertaken by the courts and judiciary, and the specific executive institutions of punishment (via the Prison Service and the Parole Board) who are responsible for how the sentence will work in practice, and how much time will be spent in or out of prison once the judicially set period of punishment has been served. The latter is not typically a judicial issue, and neither is it determined exclusively according to criteria of desert, but by weighing other factors such as the likelihood of re-offending, public safety, and the like. Viewed thus, the exercise of mercy within criminal justice has developed as a form of executive power based on very different criteria. It was, in Farmer's opinion, not on balance wrong for the Justice Minister to release and repatriate al-Megrahi on compassionate grounds.

Duff's Response to Lindsay Farmer

In his response to Lindsay Farmer's article, Anthony Duff acknowledged many of the points raised in the latter's analysis of the *al-Megrahi case*, but then went somewhat further to indicate other instances in which he perceived mercy as having a role to play in criminal justice—but in a 'broader' sense than that in which (as in the al-Megrahi instance) he held that there was a tension between mercy and justice in which the strict demands of desert became overridden by a 'merciful' impulse to an unacceptable extent. He also concurred with Farmer's view that the role of mercy is best discharged outside rather than inside the criminal court.

In doing so, Duff acknowledged that any human system of justice will be at least imperfect or 'rough' (2009b: 1-2), and that there are instances in which an offender's particular circumstances may be such that he or she does not deserve the sentence prescribed by the law, and in which an act of 'mercy' is then necessary to 'save him or her from this undeserved fate' (*Ibid.*). But here it would seem that there is a danger of confusing mercy with considerations of equity or mitigation which, from the stance adopted in this work, is both unfortunate and largely unhelpful.

Subsequently in his reply to Farmer, Duff cites the circumstances in which in England the Director of Public Prosecutions (DPP) (who must approve any prosecution for assisted suicide) will not prosecute any person who, from motives of love and compassion, helps another to travel to the Dignitas Centre in Switzerland to commit (assisted) suicide. The question that arises from this particular situation in which—at least technically—a criminal offence is committed—is whether the law is imperfect and should be amended specifically to exclude such prosecutions, or whether, in deciding not to prosecute such cases, the DPP acts justly rather than mercifully.

Finally, though somewhat earlier in his reply to Lindsay Farmer, Duff hints at the difficulties encountered in arriving at proportionality in sentencing within systems of justice that are, at best, imprecise. Though in recent years sentencing guidelines have been developed in many jurisdictions to set upper (and sometimes lower) limits on the punishment of specific offences, these guidelines may reduce, but do not eliminate sentencing disparity. At best, though the guideline limits provide space for proper consideration of mitigating and aggravating factors in relation to offences, and to some extent also confine or circumscribe notions of desert, that is all that they achieve. Decisions to sentence towards the more lenient levels of the guidelines should not, however, be confused with the exercise of mercy.

The exchange of articles between Anthony Duff and Lindsay Farmer relating to the case of Abdelbaset al-Megrahi and the Lockerbie atrocity has been of immense value to this work in identifying aspects of mercy that tend to evade rigorous attention in the considerable literature that has built up around it over the past decades. That it is a complex philosophical and practical challenge for true justice to confront is clearly evident, but if justice is to remain other than uncertain in its goals and 'rough' in operation, then the 'virtue' of mercy requires considerable de-mystification and explanation.

As to the 'rightness' or 'wrongness' of the decision made by the Justice

Minister for Scotland in the al-Megrahi context, there remains some equivocation as to precisely what factors—legal, political or humanitarian—ultimately drove it to a conclusion. If legal, then Anthony Duff's insistence that it defied the principle of desert within justice is entirely reasonable and sustainable: if political, then it was an executive decision taken for entirely extra-legal reasons entirely beyond the bounds of justice: and if humanitarian, given the seriousness of the atrocity, to what extent was it driven by doubt as to the safety of al-Megrahi's conviction in the first instance? History may never resolve this conundrum, but it is clearly questionable whether the decision was, in fact, an act of mercy.

Why is the Debate about Mercy so Important?

This chapter has outlined a number of reasons why the term 'mercy' has, over time, become confused both in its philosophical treatment within the literature relating to criminal (and civil) justice, and in its application in relation to the processes of justice delivery in an operational sense. If justice delivery is to be made less 'rough' as has been suggested earlier, and conform more closely to the principles discussed in the opening part of this chapter, then there is an evident need to re-examine its aims and purposes within our contemporary societies. If, indeed, we 'over-punish' and do so unnecessarily and at considerable social expense, then it may be the case that our processes of justice delivery are grounded in an anachronistic legacy of retributive traditionalism that militates against social cohesion in a deliberate and exclusive manner.

Re-defining mercy might enable us to re-appraise our justice processes in a more inclusive, tolerant and restorative context that would enhance both crime control and social cohesion, while at the same time giving victims of crime a proper place within considerations of justice. In order to do so, we have first to understand why the punitive legacy that we have inherited is no longer 'fit for purpose', and then work towards a form of social consensus that would better serve the needs and aspirations of a contemporary society by 'doing justice better'. In the chapter that follows, an attempt will be made to understand this punitive legacy and its effect upon the delivery of justice, and, in particular, the way in which mercy has been misconstrued in both a philosophical and an operational manner.

CHAPTER THREE

Mercy and the Punitive Legacy

Background Considerations

With the demise of the 'justice model' in the mid-and-late-1980s a vacuum was created in penal politics in Britain and the United States, and to a certain extent also in some of the countries of Western Europe—notably The Netherlands and (then Western) Germany. The domestic economies of these countries were in a state of turbulence resulting from the Arab oil crises of the 1970s, and in Britain in particular the decade of the 1980s was marked by considerable unrest and rioting in its inner-cities, the coalminers strike, the print workers dispute, the Falklands War, and the resurgence of major IRA-inspired violence in Northern Ireland and into mainland England.

The two main political parties in the United Kingdom (Conservative and Labour) were as far distanced from each other ideologically than at any time since the 1930s, with the Conservatives gaining power in 1979 under the leadership of Margaret Thatcher which was to remain held until mid-1997. The period was also one of major unrest in the prisons of England and Wales[1], culminating in the notorious riot at Strangeways Prison in Manchester in April 1990 which lasted for 25 days, and resulted in the almost complete destruction of the prison before the eyes of a worldwide viewing audience in the mass media.

The penological vacuum, for want of any alternative strategy, became filled during the 1990s by a markedly right-of-centre 'law and order' approach towards dealing with criminal offending that resulted in a rapid expansion of the prison population during the 1990s and into the new millennium.[2]

1. In April/May 1986 there were widespread disturbances in 46 prisons in England and Wales, and in 1988 major incidents at HMPs Haverigg and Lindholme (July). In May 1989 a further disturbance at HMP Risley resulted in the loss of 156 prison places, and in April 1990 a riot almost completely destroyed Strangeways Prison, Manchester with a loss of over 1,200 places.
2. In May 1988 the average daily prison population in England and Wales stood at 45,700. By May 1998 it had increased to 62,298, and by May 2008 to 82,100. It is now over 84,000.

It was also characterised by a profound change in the discourses of governmental strategies towards crime control which created a climate of despair and *anomie* amongst those working as practitioners and academic researchers in the fields of criminology and justice administration.

In his penetrating and insightful analysis of this situation in *The Culture of Control*, David Garland (2002) describes this sea-change in the following terms:

> As recently as 1970, those involved in the business of crime control shared a common set of assumptions about the frameworks that shaped criminal justice and penal practice. There was a relatively settled, self-conscious, institutional field and the debates and disagreements that occurred operated within well-established boundaries. Criminal justice textbooks and practitioner training manuals could articulate the premises that guided penal practice and confidently transmit this culture from one generation to the next. Today, for better or for worse, we lack any such agreement, any settled culture, or any clear sense of the big picture. Policy development appears very volatile, with an unprecedented amount of legislative activity, much dissention in the ranks of practitioner groups, and a good deal of conflict between experts and politicians...
>
> The constant flux and febrile energy of this transition has left an older generation of criminal justice personnel exhausted and disillusioned, cast adrift from the landmark ideals and exemplars around which they were trained. Meanwhile, their younger colleagues lack any stable ideology or conceptual framework to guide their actions or shape their visions... For at least two decades now, criminal law and penal policy have been working without clear route maps on a terrain that is largely unknown. If this field is to have any self-consciousness, and any possibility of self-criticism and self-correction, then our textbooks need to be re-written and our sense of how things work needs to be thoroughly revised (Garland, 2002:4-5).

Somewhat later in the same work, Garland added:

> For most of the twentieth century the openly avowed expression of vengeful sentiment was virtually taboo, at least on the part of state officials. In recent years explicit attempts to express public anger and resentment have become a recurring

> theme of the rhetoric that accompanies penal legislation and decision-making. The feelings of the victim, or the victim's family, or a fearful, outraged public are now routinely invoked in support of new laws and penal policies. There has been a noticeable change in the tone of official discourse. Punishment—in the sense of expressive punishment, conveying public sentiment—is once again a respectable, openly embraced, penal purpose and has come to affect not just high-end sentences for the most heinous offences but even juvenile justice and community penalties. The language of condemnation and punishment has re-entered official discourse and what purports to be the 'expression of public sentiment' has frequently taken priority over the professional judgement of penological experts (Garland, 2002 *op. cit:* 8-9).

Garland's analysis indicated above precisely summarises the situation as it was at the time that it was written. The general election of May 2010 brought back into power a Conservative /Liberal Democrat coalition government led by David Cameron which has shown no evident signs of departing from the punitive pattern of criminal justice administration that was pursued by the New Labour governments of Tony Blair and Gordon Brown that preceded it between 1997 and 2010. The average daily prison population of England and Wales remains above 84,000 in April 2014, having stood at 65,298 in May 1998, and with more than 28,000 prisoners serving sentences of four years or more, and a further 20,000 serving sentences to life imprisonment or imprisonment for public protection (IPP) on an indeterminate basis.[3]

And yet at the end of April 2012, 83 of the 134 prisons of England and Wales were officially overcrowded, holding more prisoners than their certified normal accommodation (CNA) levels permit[4] (Ministry of Justice, 2012c *op. cit.*; Prison Reform Trust, 2012 *op. cit.*: 4-5). The problem of overcrowding is exacerbated by the fact that the average tariff given for those sentenced to a mandatory life sentence has increased from 13.2 years in 2002 to 17.5

3. Source: House of Commons Library (2013), *Prison Population Statistics*, Authors: G Berman and A Dar, SN/SG/4334, London: House of Commons (29 July).
4. CNA levels represent the good, decent standards of accommodation that the Prison Service aspires to provide for all prisoners under Prison Service Order 1900. This means that widespread use is made of 'doubling-up' inmates in cells designed for single occupancy. On 23rd November 2010, Justice Minister Crispin Blunt told the House of Commons that 'we are not in a position to create enough prison places to address the problem of overcrowding' (*Hansard* HC, 23 November 2010, c155).

years in 2009, and also that by the end of March 2012, of the 6,017 prisoners serving IPP sentences 3,506 were being held beyond their tariff expiry dates (Ministry of Justice, 2012d; House of Commons, 2010).

Average sentence lengths have also increased during the past decade by the margin of 2.9 months for determinate (fixed) sentences to the extent that a median sentence to imprisonment is now of 14.8 months in duration (Ministry of Justice, 2012d; Prison Reform Trust, 2012 *op. cit.*:5). Thus, more and more persons are sent to prison for increasing periods of custody, and the penal crisis becomes 'business as usual'.

Yet all of this is markedly inconsistent with real life in the world outside the prison gates in which the volume of reported and recorded crime has decreased consistently year on year since 1995 in Britain and most of Western Europe, and the likelihood of the average citizen becoming a victim of serious injurious crime has decreased from 45% to 21.4% over the same period of time (Office for National Statistics, 2011:2; Home Office, 2011). The only plausible explanation for this state of affairs is that sentencing practices have become increasingly punitive in a retributive sense, and that desert within punishment has achieved a greater significance in assessing the blameworthiness (or culpability) of offenders.

'Populist Punitivism' and Penal Instrumentalism

The persistent trend towards increasing use of custodial punishment in pursuit of crime control is a matter of considerable concern because it is based upon largely intuitive and questionable premises that require clarification at this stage of the discussion. However, first it has to be decided whether the central and justifiable aim of criminal justice is crime *control* or crime *reduction*, since there is a tendency in many government documents—at least in England and Wales—to treat the two concepts as if they are synonymous. It is debatable whether crime control has ever been achieved anywhere, since crime is a universal fact of human existence, and to 'control' it implies doing so on a pre-emptive basis before it is actually committed. Not even the most totalitarian of social regimes has ever succeeded in such an illusory enterprise, and it remains altogether unlikely that such will ever be the case.

By way of contrast, crime reduction must logically become a possibility once offences have been committed, but only through convincing those who commit crime that to continue to do so is neither in their own interest, nor that of the wider society. Such is an educative rather than a retributive process, since it is altogether uncertain how much, or what forms of, punishment would be necessary to succeed in doing so. Recidivism statistics remind us consistently that increases in the use and duration of prison sentences fail significantly in this endeavour as matters presently stand.[5]

If, therefore, crime reduction is the main purpose of criminal justice, then continuing and increasing use of imprisonment under existing conditions is altogether unlikely to achieve it, and at a cost of £2.2bn *per annum* is also an extremely cost-intensive enterprise.[6] The average annual cost per prisoner place in England and Wales in 2012/13 was almost £38,000 exclusive of the costs of healthcare and educational provision (Prison Reform Trust, 2012a *op. cit.*:4-5; Ministry of Justice, 2012e: Table 1). The question that arises from all of this is why successive governments in England and Wales have been prepared to underwrite such expenditure at a time in which overall crime rates have been decreasing year on year since 1995.

By way of an answer to this question, it must be asserted that—as Michael Tonry pointed out a decade ago—'the bottom line is that current policies, political rhetoric and punishment patterns are as they are because politicians, however motivated, wished it so' (Tonry, 2003:6). However, in a more complex sense, during the mid-1990s and into the present decade 'Parliament enacted tougher sentencing laws, Home Secretaries (and subsequently Justice Ministers) put those tougher laws into effect, magistrates and judges sent away more people to prison and for longer times, the Parole Board became more risk averse and rates of recall and revocation of licences increased, and the probation service shifted away from its traditional supervision and social service ethos to a surveillance and risk-management ethos. In other words,

5. Prisons have a dismal record for reducing re-offending—in England and Wales 47.3% of all adults are re-convicted within one year of release, and for those serving sentences of less than 12 months this increases to 56.8%, up 2.6% since 2002. 51% of women leaving prison are re-convicted within one year, and for those serving less than one year this increases to 62%. 58% of young adults (18 to 20-year-olds) released from custody in 2008 re-offended within 12 months, and 69% of children (10 to 17-year-olds) released from custody in the 12 months ending in June 2010 re-offended within one year (Prison Reform Trust, 2012a *op. cit.*:26).
6. In real terms, total expenditure on prisons between 2003/4 and 2008/9 rose by 40% from £2.52bn to £3.98bn, including the cost of additional building, healthcare and educational provision (R Grimshaw *et al.* (2010), *Prison and Probation Expenditure 1999–2009*, London: Centre for Crime and Justice Studies, quoted in Prison Reform Trust (2012 *op. cit.*: 4-5).

every component of the English criminal justice system became tougher' (Tonry, 2003 *op. cit.*:2-3).

There are, however, other reasons for these developments which may be seen to have contributed significantly to the developments indicated above, and in a less evident manner. The rise of what Sir Anthony Bottoms described in 1995 as 'populist punitiveness' (Bottoms, 1995)—defined as allowing the perceived electoral advantage of a policy to take precedence over its penal effectiveness (Roberts *et al.*, 2003:5)—enabled politicians to claim, on a basis that was far from evidence-led, that the public were in favour of, and indeed demanded, tougher penal measures to enhance social protection and reduce the fear of crime victimisation. Indeed, in a wide-ranging review of research in this particular area of public affairs, Roberts and Stalans (1997) concluded that the public were not nearly as punitively minded as sentencers, politicians and public officials assumed them to be.[7]

In Britain during the two recent decades, the mass media have undoubtedly fuelled what is alleged to be public fear of crime and antagonism towards certain forms of offending through sensationalist treatment of crime—and most notably that of a violently sexual nature—in the tabloid press and within television coverage. Evidence in the form of crime surveys and crime statistics strongly suggest, however, that both assumed levels of public fear and the actual incidence of fear-inducing crime may be widely misunderstood by the general public, and that assumptions about its punitive dispositions are considerably overstated.

Penal instrumentalism is an entirely different matter, and one of considerable concern. It occurs, as my friend and colleague John Blad has pointed out most forcefully, when punishment is perceived as an instrument of social policy, and the limits to which it can reasonably be applied are either deliberately ignored or policies are intentionally devised to pursue an overtly punitive agenda (Blad, 2003; 2006: 137-8). In a more sinister sense, penal instrumentalism involves the use of punishment primarily as a means towards general deterrence (or prevention) and social control, and thus uses offenders as 'vehicles' by which such purposes may be achieved. Such agendas lie

7. Here see also the account of Shadd Maruna and Anna King (2004), 'Public Opinion and Community Penalties' in A E Bottoms, S Rex and G Robinson (eds.) (2004), *Alternatives to Prison: Options for an Insecure Society*, Cullompton: Willan Publishing, pp. 83-112.

beyond the notion of strict desert or proportionality, invoking a deontological approach to the use of sanctions that is irrationally at odds with its own Kantian ethical imperatives.[8]

Put another way, perhaps, penal instrumentalism represents a form of coercion that is morally questionable when it is used against persons who have committed no crime, and it uses offenders as a means of doing so. Thus to punish, in pursuit of general deterrence, beyond that extent of severity which is strictly deserved, is not only disproportionate but also vicarious and morally objectionable.

Whether we like it or not, intuitive belief in the efficacy (and indeed propriety) of general deterrence as a means of controlling crime remains deeply embedded in the handed down legacy of retributive punishment found within many of our contemporary criminal justice systems—and particularly within those that have retained Anglo-Saxon traditions of justice administration. Moreover, as Blad has further suggested:

> 'The discourse of punishment has tremendous seductive power: those willing to penalise and punish show themselves to be on the "good" side of the divide of social morality, and seem to have the courage to be tough and show the firmness needed to face the threat of crime. But unfortunately, the practices of punishment as we know them are not much less than a tragedy, especially when we consider the more serious forms of offending behaviour (Garland, 1990: 292). Punishment itself does not solve any real problems in relation to the background or causation of crime, and imprisonment as a way of punishment in most cases exacerbates the problem' (Blad, 2006 *op. cit.*: 138).

8. The term 'deontology' is derived from the Greek words for duty (*deon*) and reason or discourse (*logos*), expressing normative theories concerned with those choices that are morally required, forbidden of permitted. Such theories involve concepts of those actions that we have a moral duty to perform, amongst which in a Kantian sense, persons (unlike things) should never merely be used instrumentally as means, but rather as ends in themselves. In contrast with 'consequentialist' theories of morality that deal with the outcomes of actions, deontological ethics dictate what we have a duty to do, or the way that we should behave within the limits of our control, primarily because the consequences of actions lie in the future over which we have no control.

The Moral Credibility of the Law and the Place of Mercy

In order to operate effectively, it is widely insisted that the law has to have moral credibility in the eyes of those subject to its demands and prescriptions. Perceptions of this moral credibility may, however, vary between the social constituencies that comprise the totality of any society. What seems morally credible to politicians and policy-makers may or may not be consistent with the opinions of judges and criminal justice practitioners, of academics and researchers, of the law-abiding public, or of those who offend and become subject to the strictures of criminal justice processes.

If moral credibility is to amount to (at the least) shared perceptions of the essential 'rightness' of the law within these constituencies, then a significant extent of consensus becomes essential in relation to the relative seriousness of offences, the central purpose and propriety of sanctions, and the extent to which penalties should reasonably be imposed.[9] Retributive punishments combined with agendas of general deterrence do not sit comfortably alongside the concept of desert simply because the additional proportion of the sentence deemed necessary to deter potential offenders effectively is unknowable, but when it is aggregated with that proportion deemed appropriate in terms of retribution, the combination must exceed that strictly deserved.

Desert, in turn, is linked to the full extent of the sentence to be served, otherwise it is a meaningless concept. But it is considerably complicated by parole practices granting premature release which effectively reduce the judicially imposed sentence through executive mechanisms and decisions.[10] Deontological desert theory proposes that the state has a duty to punish offenders, and that justice is not satisfied until that process has been completed (Robinson, 2012:105). There is, therefore, an inescapable tension between desert and what are frequently, if erroneously, perceived as 'merciful' interventions that reduce the *quantum* of punishment imposed as being proportionate to moral blameworthiness or culpability (Murphy, 1986: 1).

True mercy, as we have noted in *Chapter 2*, operates outside or beyond the

---

9. In respect of the latter, the need to reduce sentencing disparity as far as possible, and uphold the principles of parsimony and of using penal custody (or deprivation of liberty) as a measure of last resort.

10. Here it will be remembered from *Chapter 2* that this was the basis of Professor Ross's objection to the release of Abdelbaset Ali al-Megrahi, although the release was on compassionate grounds rather than on parole.

judicial process as it is presently perceived, and should not be confused with mitigation which is an established element of the trial procedure. Mitigation has an important part to play in establishing levels of culpability or blameworthiness by explaining why an offender acted in the way he or she did in committing the offence(s) alleged and proven. Ultimately, evidence in mitigation is admitted to enable the court to take a more lenient view of the wrongdoing than might otherwise be the case, but it does not constitute a plea for mercy. Similarly, aggravating aspects of the offence(s)[11] that might encourage the court to take a more serious view have to be balanced against mitigating factors.[12]

Whether or not mercy should in some way be 'institutionalised' within criminal justice processes (as Robinson and some others have suggested that it might be) is perplexing if on the one hand it is not to become further confused with mitigation, or on the other it is to remain beyond the exercise of judicial discretion. As we shall see in the chapter that follows, there is a possible means by which a measure of 'institutionalisation' might be envisaged, but this could only be achieved within a restorative philosophy of justice that would require a 'paradigm shift' of the nature suggested by Randy Barnett (1977 *op.cit.*) and indicated in *Chapter 1* (*supra*). The implications of such a 'paradigm shift' are, however, far-reaching, as will become evident later in this work.

Insofar as the moral credibility of the criminal law is concerned, the nature of the consensus referred to earlier remains a critical issue. Paul Robinson has suggested that there is an inevitable tension between the exercise of mercy and the principle of treating like offences alike in relation to 'equality of desert'. It would seem to be the case that where strict adherence to equality of desert is held to be an indispensable principle in sentencing, there is no space for the institutionalisation of mercy because the two concepts become mutually exclusive and even conflicting (Robinson, 2012 *op. cit*,: 122).

Viewed somewhat differently, however, where the moral credibility of the

11. Such, for instance, as the threat or use of violence, the carriage of weapons, or the commission of offences against the elderly or children.
12. Paul Robinson (2012 *op. cit. passim*) uses the term 'mercy mitigation' extensively in his otherwise very persuasive account of the role of mercy in criminal justice. Mark Lauchs (2005 *op. cit.*:1) also cites the work of Claudia Card (1972) and Martha Nussbaum (1993) among others as examples of writers who confuse mercy with deserved mitigation (2012 *op. cit.*: 100, fn.3).

law within the community is concerned, and mercy remains a 'non-entitled' characteristic of justice,[13] the exercise of mercy may have a powerful norm-enhancing effect in 'harnessing the forces of social influence and internalised norms for more effective crime control and increase the criminal law's ability to more accurately track the community's notions of appropriate punishment' (Robinson, 2012 *Ibid.*). Robinson amplifies this proposition by suggesting that 'the more specific the articulation of the criteria for mercy, the more reliable and predictable its application and the better the system's reputation for getting it right' (*Ibid.*).

Twambly (1985: 84-90) advanced the view that mercy is only an option in civil law in which a plaintiff waives a right over a defendant, thus reducing or releasing him from an obligation which might otherwise be enforced. He further suggested that a person does not have to be in a position to punish another to show them mercy, and the person receiving mercy need not have offended the merciful person in a criminal manner. Further, Twambly pointed out that it is 'neither just to be merciful nor unjust to be merciless: refusal to grant mercy is the enforcement of a right, and the only question of justice is whether the right can be enforced. That being already decided, the court has no further role to play and cannot interfere to relieve the onerousness of the terms of the agreement.'[14]

Tasioulas (2003: 103-104) set out an entirely conflicting argument, insisting that civil matters are not merciful since they ignore his requirement that mercy must alleviate punishment. Thus civil matters relate to compensation and not to retribution, and would, therefore, consist more in simple charity since mercy relies on reason and is not just relief due to pity or other irrational causes.[15]

13. Cf. *Chapter 2* (*supra*) in that no person has a prior claim to receive mercy or forbearance, but it may be extended notwithstanding.
14. P Twambly (1985), 'Mercy and Forgiveness', in *Analysis*, vol.36, pp.84-90, quoted in M Lauchs (2005), 'Justice and Equity v. Mercy', Australian Association for Professional and Applied Ethics 12th Annual Conference, at p.3.
15. J Tasioulas (2003), 'Mercy', in Proceedings of the Aristotelian Society, vol.103, no.2, pp.101-132 also quoted in M Lauchs (2005 *op. cit.*: 4).

Alwynne Smart on 'Mercy': Clarification or Confusion?

These differences of approach to the moral credibility of the law (either civil or criminal) and mercy notwithstanding, the arguments that are entailed may be traced back to an article originally written by Alwynne Smart in 1968 in the journal *Philosophy*.[16] Smart's central premise was expressed as follows:

> A theory of punishment should give some account of mercy and yet it is true to say that very little has been said about it at all. It is commonly regarded as a praiseworthy element in moral behaviour—something practised occasionally both for the good of the one who punishes and the one who is punished. The suffering that punishment involves is unpleasant for all concerned, and if it is possible to avoid it or lessen it without moral injustice, then it is desirable to do so (Smart, 1969:212).[17]

In the body of her article Smart cited a number of different instances of offences and circumstances in which these were committed that might, in her view, merit mercy, but which, in the main, amount to matters of what would otherwise be subsumed within issues of aggravation or mitigation in considerations of punishment. These instances, she proposed were merited in order to make the punishment fit the crime in situations in which the law was too inflexible and unsophisticated to do so (Smart, 1969:217).

In her conclusion, Smart proposed that 'if we regard mercy as deciding, solely through benevolence, to impose less than the deserved punishment on an offender then the answer to the original question: when are we justified in being merciful? must be: only when we are compelled to be by the claims that other obligations have on us.' She finally suggested that mercy was a concept that only made strict logical sense in a retributive view of punishment (Smart, 1969:227).

The point of citing Smart's article here is that though it may subsequently be seen to have confused issues appearing to meet the criteria for mercy with others relating to mitigation, it prompted many subsequent attempts to define mercy and the justifications for its exercise by academics and

---

16. Smart, A (1968), 'Mercy', in *Philosophy*, vol.43, pp. 345-359. Also re-printed in H B Acton (ed.), *The Philosophy of Punishment: A Collection of Papers*, London: Macmillan, pp.212-228.
17. The reference in this instance is that which appears in Acton (1969 *op. cit.*) at page 212.

practitioners, many of whom may be seen to have fallen into the same definitional minefield. It is, however, questionably the case that as Smart insisted, the concept of mercy only makes logical sense in a retributive context of punishment. It is towards the dismantling of this particular myth that the remaining chapters of this work are devoted.

It remains evident, however, that most Western-style criminal justice systems remain locked into a retributive mode and practice of punishment from which risk-averse politicians and policy-makers are reluctant, or for reasons of perceived electoral credibility, unable to break free. In *Chapter 4* I shall attempt to sketch a pathway towards a situation in which mercy could be 'institutionalised' within a 'paradigm-shifted' concept of criminal justice administration that would accommodate just measures of retribution, though within a restorative philosophy of criminal punishment that might also maintain the moral credibility of the law.

CHAPTER FOUR

'Institutionalising' Mercy

Mercy and Retributive Penology: Incompatible Bedfellows?

In the light of what has been discussed in the preceding chapters it would be fanciful to suggest that retribution should be discarded or replaced as a distributive principle of criminal punishment. The commission of offences evidently has to have consequences, and these consequences necessarily involve measures of unpleasantness for those who offend. Since in more enlightened eras we have moved away from the infliction of physical pain on offenders (in most civilised jurisdictions), the forms that retribution takes involve the use of imprisonment (to deprive offenders of their liberty) for serious offences, and community-based sanctions for offences of lesser seriousness. The principle of parsimony suggests that punishment should be imposed to the *minimum* extent consistent with desert, and that imprisonment—as the most severe penalty—should be used only when it is strictly unavoidable.

Retribution becomes morally objectionable if or when the extent of punishment exceeds that which is deserved or justifiable, or when it is used for purposes other than as a proportionate response to offences, or when it is imposed excessively on an offender for the deliberate purpose of affecting the future behaviour of others who have not committed offences.[1] Though punishment is essentially and unavoidably an exemplary matter, its infliction on one offender in a disproportionate manner to influence or coerce the behaviour of non-offenders makes it vindictive.

If, then, retribution has to be accommodated as a penological fact of life, how may its outcomes be controlled in a manner that takes proper account

1. The latter practice is widely known within penology as general deterrence, involving the strictly excessive use of punishment of offenders to dissuade others from committing similar offences. This is a form of *vicarious* punishment used at 'second hand' as a means of social control of what is perceived to be threatening behaviour.

of true remorse in assessing desert? Does a remorseless offender deserve more punishment than a remorseful one who commits the same or a like offence? Viewed alternatively, perhaps, if the expression of true remorse is regarded as a mitigating factor for which a sentencing 'discount' is considered just and appropriate, to what extent does a remorseless attitude justify what could be termed a sentencing 'premium' as an aggravating factor? These are questions deserving of answers if retributive punishment is to be proportionate to moral blameworthiness (or culpability).

Our humane instincts seem to propel us towards a recognition that genuine remorse should not be disregarded since it expresses an extent of empathy with the person(s) offended against, and whom we term 'victims of crime'. However, a remorseful attitude may not alter the seriousness of the offence or the culpability of the offender who committed it. In an instance in which two apparently alike offences lay on the 'custody threshold' in terms of seriousness and therefore of desert, would it be justifiable to sentence a remorseless offender to imprisonment and a remorseful one to a community sanction by equitably reducing desert in the latter case?[2]

The reason for posing these questions is that we might conceive a process of jurisprudence that would be capable of dealing justly[3] with such situations without the resulting conflict of principles described above. This would involve the sort of 'paradigm shift' suggested by Barnett (1977 *op. cit.*) and discussed in the preceding chapter, while at the same time holding out the possibility of reducing the present over-use of penal custody.

Such a paradigm shift could also be envisaged within a reparative and restorative context that would give crime victims greater consideration, while also placing an emphasis on increased use of community justice. Inevitably, however, it would involve acceptance of a form of 'bifurcated justice' which I have previously described in other work (Cornwell, 2007; 2009; 2010; 2013). Such a prescription would also entail institutionalising a genuine form of mercy entirely consistent with the definitions set out earlier in *Chapter 2*.

2. Here it will be recalled from *Chapter 2* that equity was defined as displaying the means to correct or supplement the provisions of statute law by making it conform to its reason or spirit, including consideration of circumstances that reasonably necessitate or obligate leniency. However, to act in such a manner would bring justice into conflict with desert.
3. Such is to suggest ethically and fairly, and within the law in terms of its legal validity according to prescribed and accepted principles.

The question remains whether both retribution and mercy can be accommodated side-by-side within criminal justice systems. My belief is that this can be achieved if retribution is perceived merely as the 'response' to wrongdoing, stripped of suggestions of the vindictiveness evident in the 'tough on crime' mantra that has characterised criminal justice in England and Wales during the past two decades. Mercy is widely held to be the virtue that 'tempers' justice (Rainbolt, 1990; Lauchs, 2005 *op. cit.*), though there remains the belief held by some that mercy in some respects diminishes strict desert, and thereby creates injustice (Smart, 1968 *op. cit.*; Card, 1972 *op. cit.*; Hestevold, 1985 among others).

Towards an Institutionalised Form of Mercy

Mark Lauchs (2005 *op. cit.*:10) concluded his article by insisting that mercy has no place in the criminal justice system since 'all the attempts to draw a line between criminal equity and mercy fail because questions of sentencing consider when leniency should be shown and do not give a discretion whether it should be shown. Judges have a duty to apply the just outcome and any attempt to go beyond this will be invalidated by the criminal justice system and thus have no effect' (*Ibid.*). I believe that such a conclusion is erroneous since it confuses mercy with mitigation.

Paul Robinson (2012 *op. cit.*: 122) in concluding his chapter took a different view, affirming that 'the same problem does not exist for the institutionalisation of mercy when done as a means of enhancing the moral credibility of the criminal law, and thereby harnessing the normative forces of social influence and internalised norms for more effective crime control. The codification of mercy would increase the criminal law's ability to more accurately track the community's notions of appropriate punishment. The more specific the articulation of the criteria for mercy, the more reliable and predictable its application and the better the system's reputation in the community for getting it right' (*Ibid.*).[4]

The purpose of this work is to propose a model of criminal justice that would, if implemented, fulfil the following aims or purposes:

---

4. In endorsing this view I would prefer that the words 'crime control' were replaced by 'crime reduction' which seems to me to be the more appropriate and central purpose of criminal justice: a small objection, but I would suggest an important one within the context of this work.

- Enable mercy to become an integral part of a reparative and restorative justice process;
- Empower victims of crime to participate substantively in the justice process;
- Enable remorseful offenders to make reparation to victims of crime either directly or indirectly, and thereby earn their restoration to full citizenship;
- Deal equably with remorseless or intransigent offenders within a 'traditional' mode of justice which might provoke attitudinal change and empathy for victims;
- Ultimately reduce reliance upon penal custody and increase community involvement in non-custodial corrections;
- Contribute towards crime reduction and post-sentence recidivism.

Of these six aims or purposes, it will be noted that the first three posit the basis of the much needed paradigm shift discussed earlier through a new model of correctional practice for dealing with penitent offenders either in custody or in the community—and in transition from custody to the community within sentences. The latter three purposes recognise the need for prison regimes to deal with the remorseless, more serious and longer sentenced offenders some of whom might be amenable to attitudinal change, but yet in a 'traditional' setting that would encourage reform and eventual transfer to the new model at appropriate stages in longer sentences. The fifth purpose suggests the need for a much enhanced involvement of local communities in the operation of criminal justice and the arrangements for offenders serving non-custodial sentences and making reparation to victims of crime. This is an important development since the public, as taxpayers, ultimately fund the criminal justice system, and for too long have tended to regard correctional services as carried out in a 'social vacuum' in which communities have no legitimate part to play. Since most offenders return to their communities even after extensive prison custody, it is in the community interest to increase involvement and participation.

The final aim or purpose flows from those preceding it insofar as a more responsive and less remote and punitive system of criminal justice with greater use of reparative and restorative community sanctions and involvement has shown an evident potential to reduce re-offending and thus contribute to crime reduction in a cost-effective manner (Prison Reform Trust, 2102b: 7; Restorative Justice Council, 2011), and with a significant extent of victim satisfaction (Shapland *et al.*, 2011).[5] Furthermore, in 2012 the Ministry of Justice consultation with the title *Getting it Right for Victims and Witnesses* included the statement that 'the government is committed to increasing the use of restorative justice both as part of and as an alternative to the traditional model of criminal justice' (Ministry of Justice, 2012f; Prison Reform Trust, 2012b *op. cit.*: *Ibid.*). This commitment has become evident in the Crime and Courts Act 2013[6] in an amendment to the Powers of the Criminal Courts Act 2000 dealing with the deferment of sentences in respect of non-custodial sentences to allow for restorative justice interventions.

There are, therefore, signs that serious governmental attention is being devoted to restorative justice in England and Wales, though presently in the sectors of criminal justice dealing predominantly with youth offending and non-custodial sentences. With further development, the door would be opened to the full 'institutionalisation' of restorative justice interventions within criminal justice, and as will shortly be seen, creation also of the opportunity for mercy to become an integral element of that evolutionary process. First, however, the awkward issue of desert and its relationship with justice has to be dealt with.

---

5. A government funded research programme into restorative justice lasting over seven years (Shapland *et al.*, 2007) concluded that 85% of victims surveyed were either 'very' or 'quite' satisfied with their experience of restorative conferencing, and a similar proportion (80%) were found to be satisfied in the Justice Research Consortium's conferencing research. 98% of conferences ended with participants reaching an outcome agreement focused on offender reparation. Though victims tended to opt for an 'intermediary based' meeting, these led to lower levels of satisfaction than face-to-face meetings. Importantly, 27% fewer crimes were committed by offenders who had experienced restorative conferencing compared with those who did not have that experience (Restorative Justice Council, 2011; Prison Reform Trust, 2012b: 72).
6. Schedule 16 of the Crime and Courts Act 2013 at Part 2(5) provides an Amendment to the Powers of the Criminal Courts Act 2000 to enable the courts to defer the passing of non-custodial sentences to allow for restorative justice interventions (the restorative justice requirement) with the consent of the offender(s) and victim participant(s) assisted by a mediator.

Desert of Punishment

It is frequently asserted within the criminological literature that punishment is justified because the law has been broken, and that the state has a duty to maintain the moral credibility of the law by imposing penalties on those who offend. Thus, punishment is a response to crime that is both necessary and deserved. However, as Ted Honderich pointed out in his own analysis of desert claims, to say that a person deserves something and intend no more than it is right that he get it: that a man's punishment is justified by saying in this sense that he deserves it, is obviously pointless. 'Any desert claim that reduces to the assertion that it is obligatory or permissible to impose a penalty cannot, of course, be offered as a reason for the proposition in dispute, that it is obligatory or permissible to impose the penalty. This is a simple fallacy where the supposed reason is identical with the supposed conclusion' (Honderich, 1971: 26).

What is usually meant when it is maintained that a person deserves a particular penalty is that there is some relationship between the penalty and something else — most often the extent of his or her culpability or blameworthiness, the extent of the harm done, or other salient aspects of the offence, and the extent to which the offender acted intentionally or rationally.[7] However, there are other relationships that bear on this deservedness, foremost among which is that of the nature and extent of the punitive response in relation to the perceived seriousness of the offence. This is where the problems associated with desert really begin.

The notion of equivalence or proportionality dictates that for penalties to be seen to be just there must be some clearly evident correlation between offences, their relative seriousness and the punishments imposed. This supposes an ordinal relationship between offences in terms of gravity, combined with clearly defined upper and possibly lower limits within which penalties must be determined (see, e.g. Von Hirsch, 1985: 169-171 and earlier 1976; Kleinig, 1978; American Friends Service Committee, 1971 *op. cit. passim*). This much might, at least in theory, seem to be achievable: in practice, however, it has proved to be considerably more difficult in realisation. There are simple reasons for this which are evident in our day-to-day reasoning about crime and crime reduction. For instance, while there may

7. Such is to say knowingly and with an awareness that what he was doing was wrong or illegal.

be a general consensus that premeditated murder is more serious and blameworthy than manslaughter, and robbery more deserving of censure than theft, where relatively might offences of arson with intent to endanger life and aggravated rape stand within an ordinal scale of penalties?

Moreover, as Von Hirsch further argued, 'a sensible view of crime control should begin with the hypothesis that sentencing policy can, at best, have limited impact on crime rates. Insofar as anything is known about the determinants of crime, levels of criminality seem influenced chiefly by demography and by economic and social factors. These are not matters that can be altered by the state's criminal justice policies in general, or by its sentencing policies in particular. If changes in sentencing measures can enhance crime prevention at all, the impact is likely to be marginal compared to those larger influences' (Von Hirsch, 1985 *op. cit.*: 173).

There is no doubting the fact that the notion of desert or moral blameworthiness remains deeply embedded within conceptions of justice as fairness and of equity, but the difficulties evident in the 'operationalisation' of desert make it of dubious utility in decisions concerning the *quanta* of punishment or sanctions. Like theories of deterrence, it appeals to the intuitive logic of criminal punishment in an ephemeral sense, but yet it remains elusively incapable of being given practical effect as a cardinal distributive principle of justice.

All of this stated, we can describe desert adequately, and insist that to an extent that is not readily quantifiable it has a substantive effect upon sentencing decisions in relation to the seriousness of offences. If, therefore, desert of punishment is a reality with which we must live in practice, does it become too fanciful to suggest that a similar case can be made for desert of mercy? It is to this intriguing possibility that I wish now to turn attention since it could have a profound impact on the manner in which criminal justice might operate in the future.

Desert of Mercy

Recalling Alwynne Smart's insistence that a theory of punishment should give some account of mercy (Smart, 1968 and 1969: 212 *op. cit.*), and in the same sense as punishment is said to be deserved in a relationship with blameworthiness, there will arise instances within the criminal justice process in which mercy may be said to be deserved in a relationship with remorse and contrition.

It will also be recalled from *Chapter 2* that we defined mercy as a 'virtue' of justice, though one that operates outside or beyond the processes by which criminal justice is administered. Further, it was held that mercy amounts to the exercise of forbearance or compassion by one person towards another in demanding less than the full extent of severity or recompense due to, or arising from that other person's wrongful act(s) or omission(s). Mercy, therefore, is evidently a distinctly separate issue from that of mitigation which operates within the process of justice.

Within such a definition as it stands, it is evident that mercy is only exercisable once a decision has been reached as to what the penalty for the offence must be in terms of desert and severity. Institutionalisation of mercy *within* the criminal justice process implies that it should in some way be exercisable *before* a sentencing decision is made, but yet remain entirely separate from issues of mitigation. How, then, might this be achieved?

First, it would be necessary to identify cases that might qualify for considerations of mercy and separate these from those that clearly would not, and the mechanism by which such a decision could be made, and by whom. Next, it would be important to ascertain how the views of those in a position to show mercy (victims of crime) might be conveyed to sentencing officials prior to the final deliberation of the sentencing decision.[8] Within such a procedure it would normally follow that a process of mediation had taken place between the accused person(s) and the victim(s) of the offence(s) involving remorse, apology and willingness to make reparation expressed by the accused, and responded to by acceptance and some measure of forgiveness expressed by the victim (if forthcoming).

In addition, it might also be assumed that when charged with the offence the accused had formally accepted responsibility for it and indicated a willingness to plead 'guilty' and make apology and reparation if permitted to do so as a sentencing outcome. To give such a process operational effect, it would

8. In England and Wales the means of doing this already exists in the form of victim impact statements and victim personal statements (VISs and VPSs) (Cornwell, 2007:81). These can be made or updated at any stage up to the trial process, must be served upon the accused or his or her legal representative, and considered by the court in the sentencing process: *Practice Direction (Crime: Victim Personal Statements)* [2001] 4 All ER 640 : III. 28.

be necessary for an accredited and suitably trained mediator to be assigned to the case, whether the mediation procedure were to be conducted on a 'face-to-face' basis or through some form of 'shuttle diplomacy'. It would then fall to the mediator to make a report to prosecution officials indicating the outcome of the mediation process, and whether or not the victim(s) wished to appear before the court to verify the decisions agreed.

It would also seem to be appropriate that the prosecutor, taking into account the past offending record of the accused (if any) and the outcome(s) of the mediation process, should make a recommendation to the court as to whether the case should go to trial or be disposed of at a less formal summary hearing before a magistrate or a judge for a court order to be made as to the sanction and its conditions.

Within a process such as that briefly outlined above, it would be possible for cases deserving of genuine mercy to be accommodated within criminal justice systems with significant advantages in terms of time, cost and resources, and also as a means of 'institutionalising' mercy within justice. In *Chapter 5*, the implications of such a 'paradigm shift' are discussed in greater detail.

For the purposes of this chapter, however, it has been shown that there need be no necessary incompatibility between retributive justice and mercy, and also that mercy, where it is deserved, could be 'institutionalised' within criminal (and possibly also civil) processes of justice administration. As we have seen, however, the concept of desert, with its inherent difficulties and abstractions, has proved considerably less amenable to resolution other than at a somewhat vague philosophical level. For while we might conclude in given circumstances that punishment is deserved, the problems of relatively how much and how severe punishment should be in relation to different forms of offence seriousness remains elusively unresolved.

Desert of mercy is, I believe, not only an innovative concept, but also a very important one if excessive and unnecessary punishment is to be avoided. It is, however, for victims of crime to extend as both forbearance and forgiveness when (or if) they feel gracious enough to do so. It has nothing to do with mitigation of offences as we currently perceive that in operation as a means of assessing relative culpability. However, if punishment of offences is said to be deserved in some proportion to the harm caused, so, surely, is mercy deserved when the harm has been reduced or mitigated. The old English adage: 'What is sauce for the goose is sauce for the gander' has some meaning in such circumstances.

CHAPTER FIVE

Bifurcated Criminal Justice

Conceiving Corrections Differently

For the reader who is acquainted with one of my earlier works on restorative justice, *The Penal Crisis and the Clapham Omnibus* (Cornwell, 2009), this chapter will come as no particular surprise. It is, however, an updated and modified version of the proposals put forward in that work for a linked system of custodial and non-custodial corrections incorporating a 'bifurcated' custodial sector that could accommodate both those offenders requiring a 'traditional' mode of penal regime, and those deemed suitable for a more progressive, 'community-focused' and reparative form of custody split between the prison and the local community surrounding it.

The reasons for advancing such a 'paradigm shift' were outlined in *Chapter 4* in the final section dealing with 'Desert of Mercy'. Also, the need to differentiate between offenders who are remorseful and willing to make amends for their crimes, and those who are remorseless or whose offences are so serious as to make a considerable period spent in custody an unavoidable reality. In the present circumstances of criminal justice in England and Wales there is no requirement or expectation that those convicted of offences should accept responsibility for their reprehensible behaviour, or show any remorse or concern for those who became their victims. If they wish to remain remorseless or intransigent that is their choice, and they are not unduly discriminated against for doing so.[1]

On the other side of the same coin, there is no constructive process for dealing with remorseful offenders sentenced to shorter terms of imprisonment, but who are willing to accept their guilt and make apology and reparation to those offended against. These people have to endure the same

1. Other than possibly in relation to consideration for release on parole licence towards the end of longer sentences by the Parole Board, an independent body, now administered by the Ministry of Justice, and established under the Criminal Justice Act 1967 in England and Wales.

(often overcrowded) conditions and reduced regimes as those previously described, and mix with seriously criminal (and often violent or predatory) offenders sentenced to much longer terms in custody. The danger exists that these people will leave prison frustrated, bitter, sometimes traumatised, and unchanged—other than, possibly, for the worse.

Given all the evidence of numerous governmental and other reports that short prison sentences do not reduce re-offending rates (e.g. Halliday, 2001; Carter, 2003; Coulsfield, 2004; Carter, 2007), many short sentenced prisoners are sent to custody avoidably and could be better dealt with by the use of more effective non-custodial sanctions. There is thus a pressing need to re-design the present arrangements to provide more equitable justice for all the parties to this situation.

In an ideal world in which lesser resort were to be made to the use of prison custody and greater emphasis placed on community sentences and involvement, every custodial sentence of up to but less than four years, when necessarily imposed on an offender deemed amenable to the requirements of a reparative regime, should envisage that the effective sentence period be spent equally in custody and in the community.[2] This would mean that AUR and ACR sentence periods spent in custody would be halved, and ACR periods extended in all cases to provide supervision in the community (see also the last mentioned footnote) up to the expiry of the effective sentence period. The terms of ACR imply that breaches of licence conditions or commission of further offences could result in immediate recall to custody if a court so ordered.

These arrangements would probably result in sentences of less than one year being largely abandoned since the effective sentence periods would be less than six months spent equally in custody and the community. It would

2. The effective sentence period in relation to imprisonment relates to that portion of the sentence to be served in custody prior to automatic unconditional release (AUR) for sentences of less than 12 months, automatic conditional release (ACR) for sentences of 12 months or more but less than four years, and discretionary conditional release (DCR) for fixed sentences of four years or more. In all three instances the period of custody is 50% of the overall sentence period, though in ACR cases the period between 50% and 75% of the sentence is spent on licence under supervision and the remainder on unconditional release. In DCR cases the minimum period in custody is 50% of the sentence period, with a further period up to the 2/3 point spent either in prison or on discretionary release, ACR up to the ¾ point, and UCR for the remaining period of the total sentence (Criminal Justice Act 1991).

make infinitely more sense to replace the present custodial element of such sentences with a suspended sentence which could, if necessary, be activated under ACR conditions in cases of breach or further offending. In such a manner, a considerable contribution could be made to reducing the size of the prison population, and avoiding the almost meaningless use of prison custody and its undesirable effects on short sentenced prisoners and their dependents.

Such considerations notwithstanding, however, the need for a bifurcated system of criminal justice remains necessary in order to provide appropriately and separately for offenders serving reparative sentences, and those requiring the traditional pattern of imprisonment and subsequent release. The means by which this might be achieved are illustrated in *Figure 1* which has been extracted from a former work (Cornwell, 2009 *op. cit.*: 154). The diagram shows not only the potential for a 'restorative justice model' and a 'traditional' justice model to operate on a parallel (or side-by-side) basis, but also the 'crossover' points that would enable those initially sentenced to the latter form of custodial sentence to transfer to the former (restorative) model at appropriate stages of their sentences if deemed suitable and willing to do so.

From the diagram it will be noted that both the restorative and traditional models provide for non-custodial and custodial sentences, taking into account current offence seriousness and previous offence patterns, but that the reparative option is only available within the restorative model for those suitable and willing to follow it either initially in custody, or having been given a community sanction. The traditional model also offers an opportunity for offenders released under parole licence conditions to opt to complete a reparative community service element in place of remaining under parole conditions. Such a provision might be of particular benefit to those serving long prison sentences in traditional custody, many of whom experience the greatest difficulty in gaining employment on release, and also assist in their reintegration and resettlement within their communities.

The nature of the arrangements described briefly above indicate that it would be desirable for certain prisons to be designated as reparative prisons, or at least entirely separate parts of larger prisons with work and training facilities that would enable inmates to undertake a full eight hour working day to earn realistic wages from which deductions would be made to compensate victims of crime. It would also be necessary for such prisons to have 'hostel-type' accommodation and catering provision for those inmates working in the community from custody to return to each evening under secure supervision. Moreover, in the event that reparative custody estate was provided within the perimeter of large prisons operating in a traditional mode, it would be essential to separate the two modes securely to ensure that contraband items could not be traded between them, and thus prevent the pressures of 'contamination' from affecting the operation of reparative regimes.

The structure necessary for effective delivery of community sanctions would involve the establishment of a network of centres that could be coterminous with existing probation areas, and which would work in conjunction with local community justice forums to generate work programmes and projects identified by the local community as of amenity value that could not otherwise be provided within existing financial or logistical civic resources. It would be important for these projects to be constructive and skills-imparting to produce high quality outputs, while at the same time enhancing the longer term employability of the offenders assigned to them under the supervision of qualified and approved instructors. The same centres could also provide a base for the delivery of rehabilitative programmes and counselling to ensure that the social deficits of offenders were addressed in conjunction with working to make reparation.[3]

Funding for expanded and re-modelled community corrections could be made available largely from the reduction in prison places, since community sanctions are significantly less expensive than the costs of imprisonment.[4]

---

3. Social deficits of many offenders include drug and alcohol addictions, behavioural problems including aggressiveness and the need for anger management counselling, parenting problems and the like, for which cognitive programmes are available and could be delivered under Probation Service arrangements and supervision.
4. In 2011/12 the average annual cost per prisoner place was £37,618, and in 2008/9 the cost of short (less than 12 months) sentences was £286m. Balanced against these costs, that of a high-intensity two year community order including 80 hours of unpaid work and mandatory accredited programmes was £4,200 (National Audit Office, 2010). The average cost in legal and court fees of imposing a Crown Court sentence in 2010 was £30,500 (All Prison Reform Trust (2012b *op. cit.*:5-6)). Here see also: National Audit Office (2010), *Managing Offenders on Short Custodial Sentences*, London: NAO for further cost comparisons.

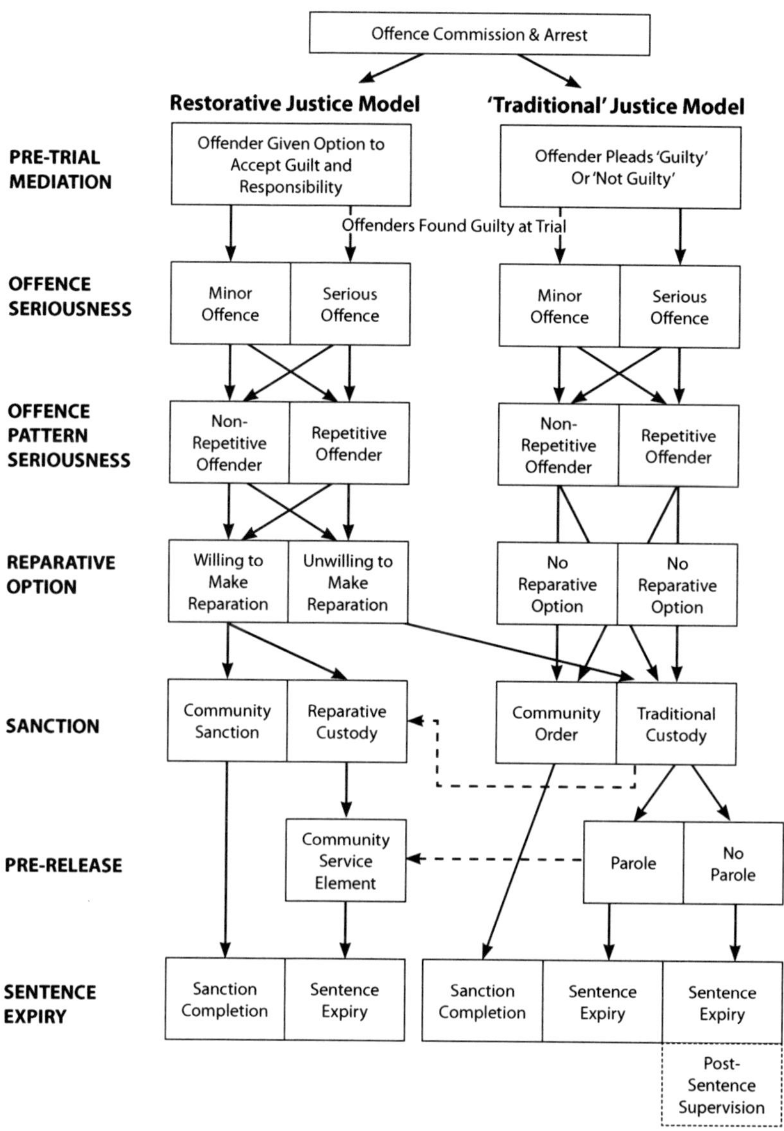

Figure 1: A Bifurcated Model of Criminal Justice

In addition, court ordered community sentences are more effective by eight percentage points at reducing one-year proven re-offending rates than custodial sentences of less than 12 months for similar offenders. Offenders discharged from immediate custodial sentences in 2008 also committed more re-offences than matched offenders given a community order, with a difference of 80.3 re-offences per 100 offenders (Ministry of Justice, 2010).[5]

Since all these facts are in the public domain, it remains all the more surprising that in an era of considerable national economic and fiscal uncertainty these unnecessary costs are perpetuated in England and Wales without apparent questioning and objection. In similar circumstances other nations such as Finland, Germany, The Netherlands, France, Canada and certain states within the USA have taken decisive action to reduce the use of imprisonment as an unnecessary and inappropriate waste of economic resources (Cornwell, 2007 *op. cit.*: 165-6; Tonry, 2003 *op. cit.*: 212). In almost every case, such action was accompanied by no significant increase in the volume of recorded crime or rates of re-offending. The inevitable question which arises from such a situation is that of why it has not been addressed in England and Wales which have endured a deepening penal crisis since the mid-1990s.

Objections to Bifurcated Penal Policies

Though it is probably true to assert that the concept of bifurcation has never been given serious consideration in England and Wales as a means of reducing the prison population and, at the same time, of providing better justice for offenders, victims and communities, there are a number of reasons why this may be the case. Some of these reasons are strictly political, others lie within the structure of the criminal justice system, and yet more are attributable to misconceptions of crime held by the public as a result its treatment within the mass media. I shall deal with each of these sources of objection briefly in turn, and attempt to provide some explanation as to how they have become prevalent.

At the national political level, in countries that are governed under what is effectively a bi-partisan system with no substantial competition from a third party of reckonable electoral potential, or a combination of smaller parties that could form a viable coalition in opposition, there is an inevitable tendency towards policy stagnation and even convergence. Politicians placed in such circumstances become risk-averse and ultra-cautious in relation to innovative ideas and initiatives for fear of failure and consequent loss of political credibility, and therefore of power. They also become extremely

5. Ministry of Justice (2010), *Compendium of Re-offending Statistics*, London: Ministry of Justice; Prison Reform Trust (2012a *op. cit.*: 26).

'media-conscious' and concerned with issues of 'image', and reluctant—both individually and collectively—to adopt stances of principle which might attract adverse reaction from their electoral constituencies or party supporters, or from the general public however misinformed or uninformed.

It is also a truism that certain 'issues' of genuine public interest or concern tend to dominate both the political and social discourses of each generation, and to a greater or lesser extent which can change quite rapidly at times of perceived crisis or uncertainty. High on the agenda of such issues are those of public safety, crime prevention and personal risk that threaten the stability of relatively affluent societies. Those members of these societies who pose a threat of criminal activity or public risk can therefore 'legitimately' be marginalised and preferably neutralised. Why they behave in such a manner is of much lesser importance than that they be prevented rather than dissuaded from doing so. The result is the development of policies of incapacitation for public protection.

Within the structure of criminal justice, reluctance to adopt policies of bifurcation has been justified predominantly on the grounds that the practice infringes the principle of treating like offences in a like manner. Put another way, perhaps, it is objected that by selecting certain offenders for reparative sanctions while others who commit similar crimes are dealt with traditionally, creates an injustice that is inequitable. The objection is, I would maintain, questionable. The reason for this is that the principle of parsimony demands that punishment be imposed at the least extent consistent with culpability or desert, and that levels of culpability differ considerably between remorseful and remorseless offenders. Therefore, to punish both identically in terms of extent would be an injustice done to the remorseful.

Politics and Public Opinion

It is frequently asserted by politicians anxious to maintain a 'tough on crime' stance in relation to offenders and 'would be' offenders that the public demands or expects relatively harsh sentences for certain forms of offending, and in particular those of a violent and/or sexual nature or committed against children or the elderly. Media, and in particular tabloid sensationalism of such offences 'talks up' the punitive rhetoric, while at the same time fuelling or encouraging a supposed public fear of crime or victimisation that is disproportionate to its actual prevalence. Thus the suggestion that certain offenders considered amenable to reparative sanctions should be afforded the opportunity to be dealt with in a restorative mode of justice feeds the belief that they are being dealt with in an unacceptably lenient manner.

Considerable research has been devoted to the study of public opinion in relation to crime and punishment (see, e.g. Maruna and King, 2004 *op. cit.*: 83-112), much of it with somewhat equivocal outcomes partly due to differences in research design. Such consensus as there is seems to indicate that public attitudes towards the treatment of criminals are generally less punitive than might be thought to be the case, although public understanding of the workings of the criminal justice system is variable and frequently distorted by the extensive treatment of crime in the media, and an apparently insatiable appetite for 'real life crime drama' in televised form. This has resulted in what Cullen *et al.* (2000) have described as a somewhat 'mushy' situation that can be interpreted quite differently by politicians and policy-makers, criminologists and penal reformers, depending on the agendas adopted for crime control legislation.

The question remains largely unresolved as to whether policies of penal bifurcation are genuinely objectionable in principle, or rather whether such policies are a logical resort if it were to become evident that crime reduction and lesser recidivism would result from them. This work holds to the latter approach simply because the stalemated situation within criminal justice in England and Wales is now so much 'business as usual' and unacceptable when viewed in the light of the evident success of the 'reductionist' initiatives adopted by other Western European nations.

Bifurcation, however, requires a consensus between politicians, the judiciary, policy-makers, academics, penal system practitioners and the media that its potential benefits extend beyond the partisan interests that so frequently stifle reform and progress in many areas of public life. It requires a *quantum* change in sentencing practices, a willingness to admit victims to a substantive place within the justice process, and an infrastructure that would enable a considerably increased participation by communities in supervising and delivering its outcomes in terms of reparative work done by offenders. Bifurcation also has the potential to reduce the collateral damage presently caused by over-use of imprisonment to the immediate dependants and families of offenders sentenced to custody unnecessarily.

Paradoxically, public confidence in corrections tends to decline when re-offending rates are seen to be high. The fact that imprisonment clearly fails to deter more than half of all those thus sentenced, and in particular to sentences of 12 months or less, from being re-convicted within a year of release (Prison Reform Trust 2012b *op. cit.*:26) is predominantly due to the fact that resources are insufficient to address their offending behaviour because of the pressures of overcrowding and the short effective lengths of their sentences. As we have noted previously, however, community sentences are considerably more effective than imprisonment in reducing re-offending, and should therefore logically be used to a greater extent than at present. Bifurcation policies, if adopted, would enable considerable numbers of less serious offenders to be diverted from custody, while at the same time reducing the pressure on prison places.

Lack of purposeful employment and skills deficits are a major factor in encouraging recidivism, particularly among the younger (18 to 25 year-old) sector of offenders, the majority of whom express a wish to stop offending (Ministry of Justice, 2010 *op. cit.*: 26). Community sanctions involving planned and supervised work projects can be an important means by which skills training can be made available, increase offender employability, and therefore contribute to crime reduction. Once again, bifurcation would assist in achieving this desirable outcome.

Reparative Sanctions and Victim-Offender Mediation

Finally, the fact that reparative sanctions encourage mediation between offenders and victims to the widely felt benefit and understanding of both parties to offences, means that a dialogue is opened up with mutual potential advantages. Offenders have the opportunity to accept responsibility, make apology and offer reparation, while victims may be encouraged to extend a measure of forgiveness to offenders and request that less severe sentences be imposed upon them than might otherwise strictly be deserved. The fact of their inclusion and participation in such a process of reconciliation would enable victims to feel vindicated, while at the same time giving them a recognised stake within the criminal justice process.

Communities also have a legitimate interest as stakeholders in the outcomes of sanctions, most particularly in reduced recidivism and in the potential amenity value of reparative work completed by offenders. Where this becomes fully effective in practice, there is an increased likelihood that public opinion will become more accepting of the appropriateness of community-based sanctions as alternatives to the wasteful practice of imprisonment. It is, however, victims of crime who deserve the primary consideration as those harmed by criminal acts.

In *Chapter 6* we shall examine what might be described as the legitimate claims of crime victims to receive due recognition of their status, become stakeholders within criminal justice, and extend mercy to offenders when it is appropriate and helpful for them to do so.

We will also examine the concept of victim personal statements (VPSs) and victim impact statements (VISs) admissible in the courts of England and Wales since 2001 and mentioned briefly in *Chapter 4, supra*, with a view to determining the extent to which that initiative meets or conflicts with the purpose of delivering true criminal justice.

CHAPTER SIX

Victims of Criminal Justice?

The nature of the debate

The status of victims within contemporary criminal justice in England and Wales is, to say the least, equivocal. How this situation is viewed depends considerably upon whether the purpose of the system of justice administration is perceived as primarily retributive or potentially restorative in nature. If the former, the focus is on the punishment of offenders on the basis of desert (or culpability), and victims become a peripheral consideration: if the latter, then victims have an expectation of inclusive consideration, and offenders have an evident responsibility to make reparation for the harm caused by their offences.

If the central purpose of criminal justice is to restore the social equilibrium disturbed by crime, then this is essentially a prospective motivation: if, however, it is to repay those who offend with a measure of reciprocal unpleasantness, then punishment becomes predominantly retrospective and focused on the wrongful act—saving that if it is also imposed to deter the offender and/or those who might offend similarly from so doing, it might be said to have a secondary and questionably uncertain forward-looking aim.[1]

As matters presently stand, there is no particular expectation that offenders should show any genuine remorse for their crime, or, indeed, any concern for those offended against. If they decline to do so, then the notion of proportionality requires that they be punished strictly according to the seriousness of their offence(s) because the law has been broken and the punishment is, therefore, deserved. The victims of the crimes of unrepentant offenders thus become marginalised in the primary interest of justice being seen to be

1. Uncertain because it is difficult to be precise about how much unpleasantness would be necessary to achieve this purpose, or, indeed, whether it has subsequently been effective in operation. Perhaps more objectionably, if punishment is to be said to be proportionate to desert—however that is calculated—then the additional 'premium' imposed to encourage deterrence (whether individual or general) renders it disproportionate and arbitrary.

done. The question therefore arises as to whether such a process of justice is morally defensible other than in a specifically retributive sense.

Restoring the social equilibrium disturbed by crime supposes at least an extent of community involvement, the purpose of which should be devoted to the reconciliation of those offended against with those who cause them offence. This implies a multi-dimensional view of crime not only as an infraction of the law, but also as a breach of the social order affecting both victims, communities and offenders and those dependent on them. A purely retributive response to crime may serve to satisfy the demands of the law, but it largely neglects the social stakeholders whose legitimate interests the law is designed to protect. Such a mono-dimensional view of crime is ultimately more socially divisive than inclusive, and on this ground morally questionable—at least in a utilitarian sense.

This raises the somewhat interesting and complex further question of whether a restorative philosophy of criminal justice, inclusive of victims and communities, necessarily implies a predominantly utilitarian perspective in relation to crime and punishment. That, I believe, goes beyond the deontological *versus* consequentialist debate espoused by commentators such as Larry Alexander and Michael Moore (2007 and 2012) for reasons that require brief explanation here.[2] For if the central purpose of criminal justice is met and satisfied entirely through the duty of the state to punish offences according to desert, then the collateral (or consequential) damage to the social wellbeing may be set aside as a tangential, or at least, a secondary consideration. To behave in such a manner opens the door to a form of penal instrumentalism, using offenders as the means towards social control rather than as ends in their own interests of restoration, and those of social harmony and cohesion.

But if, on the other hand, the dominant purpose of criminal justice is to promote and maintain the safety and security of populations and of the communities within them while at the same time reducing crime, then the ultimate restoration of offenders to a 'good and useful life'[3] through remorse,

2. Here see: Alexander, L and Moore, M (2007/2012 Rev.), 'Deontological Ethics', *The Stanford Encyclopedia of Philosophy*, E N Zalta (ed.) (Winter 2012 edition). An online (27pp) version of the revised article is available at http://plato.stanford.edu/entries/ethics-deontological/.

3. The reference here is to the text of the former Prison Rules 1964 in England and Wales [SI 388], Rule 1 of which stated that: 'The purpose of the training and treatment of convicted

apology and reparation becomes a transcendent motivation over punishment alone.[4] Though such an approach has a moral justification on consequentialist grounds, the ends being more important than the means, it remains awkwardly at odds with the imperative deontological notion that punishment must be seen to be the axiomatic and proportionate response to crime on the basis of desert because the law has been broken.[5]

The Approach of Cavadino and Dignan (1997)

Addressing these difficulties in 1997, two widely respected British criminologists Michael Cavadino and James Dignan identified five different models of criminal justice and of reparation's relationship to the criminal justice system (Cavadino and Dignan, 1997: 233-253). The first of these models was that of 'conventional' (or traditional) criminal justice as practiced in England and Wales over decades past, with its essentially retributive reliance on just deserts, providing limited potential for reparation to victims in any form other than the compensation order, and largely neglecting them other than as potential witnesses. The second model was one involving 'victim allocution' in which the wishes of victims might be influential (or even paramount) in decisions to prosecute and/or concerning sentencing—either through victim impact statements or as witnesses. A third model was of a 'welfare'-based nature incorporating support and assistance for victims, though detached from the criminal justice system, making victims supplicants or claimants within state-funded schemes.

The fourth model they described as an imaginary 'strictly proportionate

---

prisoners shall be such as to encourage them to lead a good and useful life.' Home Office (1964), *The Prison Rules*, SI 388 in pursuance of section 47 of the Prison Act 1952, London: HMSO. These Rules were superseded in 1999.

4. Here, of course, it might be said that the utilitarian motivation of avoiding or reducing mischief is strongly evident. However, the means by which this might be achieved have unfortunately strong links with theories of general deterrence, and thus with disproportionate punishment (Bean, 1981: 39-40; Honderich, 1976 *op. cit.*: 84-86).
5. The difficulty with both deontological and consequentialist theories of morality is that both contain evident strengths and weaknesses. These are explained at some length in Alexander and Moore's (2012) account, and yet both theories seem resistant to absolute separation, having 'blurred' boundaries that enable each account to accommodate the other to a limited extent. I use them here, however, as illustrative of the dichotomous debate within penology as to the ultimate purpose of criminal punishment, and therefore of the differences that separate the retributive and restorative positions in this regard.

composite' "straw" model' which was predominantly retributive with limited potential for reparation, though including compensation orders and a form of 'individual service order'. This model was assisted by local reparation services, and permitted possible victim involvement in negotiation with a limited choice of reparative packages. The fifth and final model was what was described as an 'integrative restorative justice model', fully-focused on reparation by, and the reintegration of offenders, administered by local reparation services and using the courts only in the prosecution and enforcement roles. The model would, however, permit the active involvement of victims in negotiations preceding formal decisions on prosecution or sentence, and was the model of their choice.[6]

Leaving on one side the evident disadvantages and limitations of the first four models outlined above, the fifth most closely resembles the stance taken within this work. This model does, however, contain some proposals that extend beyond the scope of the nature of the restorative justice model adopted in this work, most particularly in relation to the status of the courts and the extent to which victims might participate within the process of trials.

Victim Status: The Need for Caution

Though the present situation of victims within the criminal justice system of England and Wales is evidently unsatisfactory and lacking in empowerment, there are issues of principle that need to be addressed in deciding upon the extent to which their participation in trial processes and outcomes is reasonable or acceptable. These issues relate predominantly to decisions over prosecution, differences between evidence and statements of 'feeling and situation', and 'interference' in the sentencing deliberations of the courts.

As the aggrieved parties to offences it is natural and expectable that victims will hold strong views about their own experiences and those of close others affected within their communities.[7] A balance has therefore to be reached

6. For a summary chart indicating the full extent of these models see: Cavadino, M and Dignan, J (1997), 'Reparation, Restitution and Rights' in *International Review of Victimology*, vol.4, pp.233-253, but especially here p.234.
7. The term 'community' here is used in the sense of differing forms of affiliation including immediate families, neighbourhood relationships and the wider social structure within which these are integral elements. Serious crimes, while deeply affecting victims, immediate families and neighbourhoods also achieve national publicity, arousing public and political reaction that can jeopardise the fairness of trial processes due to excessive or sensationalist media exposure

in deciding the extent to which victims themselves (rather than their legal representatives) should become involved in the aftermath of offences, in deliberations over the prosecution of alleged offenders, and within subsequent trial procedures. It is also essential that accused persons are treated fairly and equably, and are not subjected to discrimination which can arise from differences in victim reaction or wider perceptions of the seriousness of alleged offences.

Generally speaking, when an offence is alleged and brought to the notice of the police with sufficient evidence to render it substantial, the offender should be charged with its commission and a decision made as to its prosecution or other admissible disposal.[8] In the interests of parity as between cases and alleged offenders of a similar nature, it is undesirable that victims should participate in this decision-making process other than strictly as witnesses. Victim impact statements (VISs),[9] where submitted, are not considered in prosecution decision-making.

It is at this stage that proponents of models of restorative justice reparative processes are likely to encounter, and have to overcome, the first serious *tranche* of objections to their agenda. In recent years it has become a feature of these models—as Cavadino and Dignan (1997 *op. cit.*:236-7) have shown—to propose the need for a mediation process to be available prior to decisions being made as to prosecution. The purpose of this process would be to ascertain the views of victims as to whether or not they wished a prosecution to proceed, or rather, whether in the event that apology and reparation were to be offered by the offender, they would be content to accept and even consider extending forgiveness to some or another extent.

---

and commentary.

8. In relation to many minor offences in most jurisdictions the police have a power and discretion to issue formal cautions or warnings. Where more serious offences are alleged, national justice systems differ in procedures leading to decisions as to prosecution made by prosecutors, examining magistrates or other similarly appointed officials.

9. Also known as victim personal statements (VPSs). Where permitted these are not designed to influence decisions in relation to prosecution, but are made for the information of the judge or magistrates after a finding of guilt has been reached at trial, to be considered in the sentencing process. Submission of a VPS or VIS does not preclude a victim appearing as a witness if so required by the prosecution.

The Objections of Andrew Ashworth (1992 and 1993)

Critics of such proposals such as Andrew Ashworth (1992) have objected to such an arrangement as a matter of principle, insisting that victims should have no special say (over and above that of any other member of the public) as to whether an offender should be prosecuted or not (1992:10). Such decisions, in the view of Ashworth and others, are the domain of prosecuting authorities, and should properly be reached entirely on the basis of the evidence available.

The basis of the objection raised by Ashworth and others of a similar view rests on three main points. First, that whatever the feelings of the victim may be, a prosecution may be in the 'public interest' and should, therefore, be pursued. Second, that to consider victim's views at that stage in the justice process risks a conflict with the principle of punishment in accordance with 'just deserts'. And thirdly, that any decisions made on such a basis may lead to inconsistencies of treatment as between offenders in relation to the individual inclinations of prosecutors or the idiosyncrasies of particular judges or magistrates (1992:10).

Proponents of a mediation process at an early stage within a restorative justice model hold to the view that offenders who are prepared to accept responsibility for the harm they have caused, make apology and offer reparation, should be enabled to do so through a mediated process involving victims either directly or through an approved third party. This, they insist, should logically take place prior to a decision over prosecution being made because the offender has accepted guilt, and therefore resort to a full trial hearing might be unnecessary and save much time and expense 'in the public interest'. Moreover, such proponents would also assert that victims have a status and interest quite different from 'any other member of the public', and that consequently their wishes should be at least considered by prosecutors as the outcomes of an approved mediation process.

Accepting that the objection of Ashworth and others has some weight in principle, as did the objection of Professor Ross in the *al-Megrahi case* (*Chapter 2, supra*), the more important question seems to be that of which approach delivers better and fairer justice. Prosecutors (or examining magistrates) are experienced and trained public officials whose decision-making powers are circumscribed by guidelines and precedent, and whose conduct is subject to scrutiny and oversight. They are also entrusted to work in the public interest in a professional manner. At some stage in the process it has to be decided whether the remorse shown by offenders is genuine or contrived, and weigh this and the wishes of victims against the seriousness of alleged offences which may, indeed, demand prosecution in the public interest and thus render the cost-benefit consideration redundant.

Furthermore, determination of desert in relation to culpability becomes a matter for consideration once a finding of guilt has been arrived at, based on the evidence available to the court. Where guilt is accepted *ab initio*, only seriousness, mitigation and aggravation remain to be decided by those concerned with sentencing—regardless of whether the accused pleaded 'guilty' or 'not guilty', or changed his or her plea in the interim. It would therefore seem that Ashworth's objection in relation to desert can be accommodated within the sentencing process of a restorative justice model as appropriately as within the traditional (or 'justice' model) that he evidently espouses.

This brings us to the contentious issue of the extent to which victims should properly be included in the process by which decisions are made about the punishment of offenders convicted of offences within a primarily reparative and restorative model of justice. Here, Ashworth's objections require serious consideration since he raises a matter of fundamental procedural importance which is much more difficult to refute. In his own words, he insists that 'the provisions of the criminal law set out to penalise those forms of wrongdoing which touch on public rather than merely private interests' (1992:3) and that 'punishment is a function of the state, to be exercised in the public interest' (1993:284).[10]

Though it has been conceded earlier that the views and wishes of victims should properly be taken into account in decisions as to prosecution, the issue here is whether victims should have a right to address the court (victim 'allocution') when sentencing is considered, in addition to, or instead of being able to submit a victim impact statement (or VPS). Ashworth is implacably opposed to such a development, particularly in relation to matters concerning the severity (or otherwise) of punishment: a stance supported within this work, and also by Cavadino and Dignan (1997 *op. cit.*:238). The main reason for this reluctance is that victims have the opportunity to appear as witnesses

10. Quoted in Cavadino and Dignan (1997 *op. cit.*:237).

as to evidence, and to extend their participation to 'allocution' would place them in an exceptional situation which is not permitted to other persons within sentencing deliberations.

Two further issues also bear on this situation. In instances in which a mediated outcome has been reached and agreed when an offender has accepted guilt and offered reparation, the views of victims will already have been taken into account in decisions as to prosecution, and therefore, a further participation would be largely superfluous. However, if an offender pleads 'not guilty' and yet is convicted, issues of aggravation and mitigation are taken into consideration prior to sentencing, and in assessing culpability or desert. The danger is that further involvement of victims ill-disposed towards the offender and not subject to cross-examination might unduly 'skew' sentencing decisions, and thus result in injustice and unfairness. Thus, victim 'allocution' becomes a contentious issue best avoided in the interests of doing justice.

The restorative justice reparative model proposed within this work is in some respects similar to the integrated restorative justice model suggested by Cavadino and Dignan (1997 *op. cit.*:234), though with some important differences. It is represented in *Figure 2* later in this chapter by way of contrast with the 'traditional' retributive model discussed earlier. While the philosophy and main aims of this model are broadly similar to that of Cavadino and Dignan's integrated model, the institutional framework in which it is set lies firmly *within* the existing criminal justice system, and the role of victims within it is somewhat more limited than that envisaged by those authors.[11]

It is of interest to note here that Cavadino and Dignan's integrated model apparently placed its reparative provisions *outside* the formal criminal justice process, under the *aegis* of local reparation services, and proposed using prosecution and the courts mainly in an enforcement capacity. In so doing, it must be assumed that they perceived a mediated settlement including reparation as being somewhat similar to an 'out of court' settlement in a civil dispute, to be prosecuted only in default by recourse to the criminal courts. Quite why they did so is left unclear, since such a position causes some difficulty in relation to the recording of convictions, and of any additional penalties

11. The model contrived by Cavadino and Dignan (1997 *op. cit.*) included the active participation of victims in negotiations preceding formal decisions on prosecution *or* sentence, even though the authors did not favour victim 'allocution' (1997 *op. cit.*: 234 and 238).

or conditions that the courts might otherwise wish to impose on offenders.[12]

Victims' Rights: Myth or Reality?

The past two decades in Britain and elsewhere in Western Europe have witnessed a considerable upsurge of interest in victims' 'rights', but few substantive expressions of what these rights actually amount to in practice. Indeed, definitions of 'rights' differ widely, depending upon the contexts in which they arise.[13] Rights are also linked with responsibilities on the part of the holder and those from whom a corresponding duty or obligation is required. The entire concept of rights is complex, having generated a considerable volume of its own literature in both an historical and a contemporary setting. For the purposes of this work, however, it is important to discern the extent to which victims of crime can be said to have 'rights', and what the nature of these rights actually amounts to in practice. Moreover, if rights invoke corresponding responsibilities, it becomes necessary to identify whose these responsibilities are, and the extent to which the rights should be enforceable and by whom.

In a context such as that in which victims of crime find themselves having been wronged or harmed, frequently on an entirely involuntary basis and through no particular fault of their own, theoretical 'rights' become of dubious value in resolving their situation. In the present circumstances of criminal justice in Britain in particular, it is difficult for victims to assert such 'rights' as they might have because the legal context in which these rights should arise is, as we shall see, equivocal or at the least ambivalent. The debate concerning 'victim allocution' is clear evidence that such is the case. In addition, the argument in favour of substantive victims' 'rights' is not reducible to considerations of compensation alone since its context is of a much wider nature that involves the responsibilities or duties that might be claimed to be owed by the state, offenders and communities to victims

12. Such, for instance, as orders to undergo various forms of addiction or behavioural counselling, or report at intervals to a supervising probation officer as provided for in the existing community order in England and Wales.

13. Rights are widely defined as legal, social or ethical (moral) principles of freedom or entitlement, or the fundamental normative rules about what is allowed of people or owed of people, according to some legal system, social convention or ethical theory. See here, for example, L Wenar (2011), 'Rights', in *Stanford Encyclopedia of Philosophy*, E N Zalta (ed.) (Fall 2011 edition), at: http://plato.stanford.edu/entries/rights/

of crime in both a social and a legal sense.

The Victim's Charter 1990 and Onwards

The Victim's Charter originally devised and published in 1990,[14] revised in 1996,[15] and reviewed in 2001,[16] remained an initiative without legal force in spite of what might have been assumed from its various sub-titles. Then in 2005, following a period of consultation, a new document with the title: *The Code of Practice for Victims of Crime* was published (Home Office, 2005b, *op. cit.*), immediately preceded by a further document bearing the title: *Victims' Rights* (Home Office, 2005a *op. cit.*). In terms of enforceability, the latter document provided little of substance other than a number of provisions relating to what victims might 'expect' in their situation.[17] The same document made no specific reference to a right to have the post-crime circumstances of victims considered in the sentencing process[18], or to any governmental intention to implement a concept of offender reparation to victims of crime.

Following upon this apparent flurry of interest in victims, there then came a period of almost deafening silence on the subject until in January 2012 the Ministry of Justice published a Consultation Paper: *Getting it Right for Victims and Witnesses* under the signature of the Lord Chancellor and Secretary of State for Justice (Ministry of Justice, 2012f *op.cit.*).[19] Once again, this paper avoids mention of victims' 'rights', but deals much more with services to

14. Home Office (1990), *Victim's Charter: A Statement of the Rights of Victims*, London: HMSO.
15. Home Office (1996), *Victim's Charter: A Statement of Standards for Victims of Crime*, London: HMSO.
16. Home Office (2001), *A Review of the Victim's Charter*, London: Home Office Communications Directorate.
17. These 'provisions' included the 'right' to be informed about their crime within specified time-scales, and of any arrests or court cases; the 'right' to clear information on compensation and on eligibility under the Criminal Injuries Compensation Scheme; the 'right' to be informed if they are required as witnesses; an 'entitlement to help and advice from the charity Victim Support; and the 'right' to be informed (in cases in which an offender is imprisoned for longer than one year) of his or her release from custody. It was further made explicit that the victim's right to privacy and the media's right to freedom of expression are both set out within the Human Rights Act 1988.
18. Through, for instance, an absolute requirement of those passing sentence to consider any submission made by a victim in the form of a VPS (or VIS) or similar document. It will be recalled from earlier discussion, however, that the *Practice Direction* issued by the Lord Chief Justice in October 2001 had made specific provision for this to be done.
19. Consultation Paper CP3/2012, CM 8288.

victims and witnesses, and the means by which these can be funded within existing resources.

Somewhat touchingly, in the final paragraph in the Foreword to the 2012 Paper, the Lord Chancellor states:

> Victims are too often an afterthought for the criminal justice system. But they are the people to whom we have the greatest responsibility. Their needs should be dealt with sensitively, proportionately and promptly. I believe the proposals in this paper will ensure victims' services are on a sustainable footing and go a long way to putting right the failings of the past (Ministry of Justice, 2012 *op. cit.*: 4).

But for all of this, the rights of victims remain a mythical construct within criminal justice in England and Wales as matters presently stand. In spite of all the rhetoric, it seems as though the issue of giving victims of crime rights is almost delicately avoided for some fear of the consequences of insisting upon doing so. This is strange in a democracy in which crime victims are (or should be) uniquely placed to extend mercy to truly penitent offenders, given a sensitive and properly recognised environment in which to do so. Since the exercise of forgiveness can also help to heal the trauma of victim status, it remains a grievous anomaly that the rights of victims remain so ambiguously neglected.

In the chapter that follows we shall examine the nature of rights within the literature on that subject, in an attempt to discern why the rights of victims of crime appear to be so problematic. If this situation could in some way be resolved, then the prospect of a more merciful and less retributive system of criminal justice might become capable of realisation. At this stage, however, it might be suggested that continued failure to enable this trauma to be reduced, in combination with that of denying the specification of actual rights, contributes significantly towards making victims of crime victims also of the criminal justice system itself.

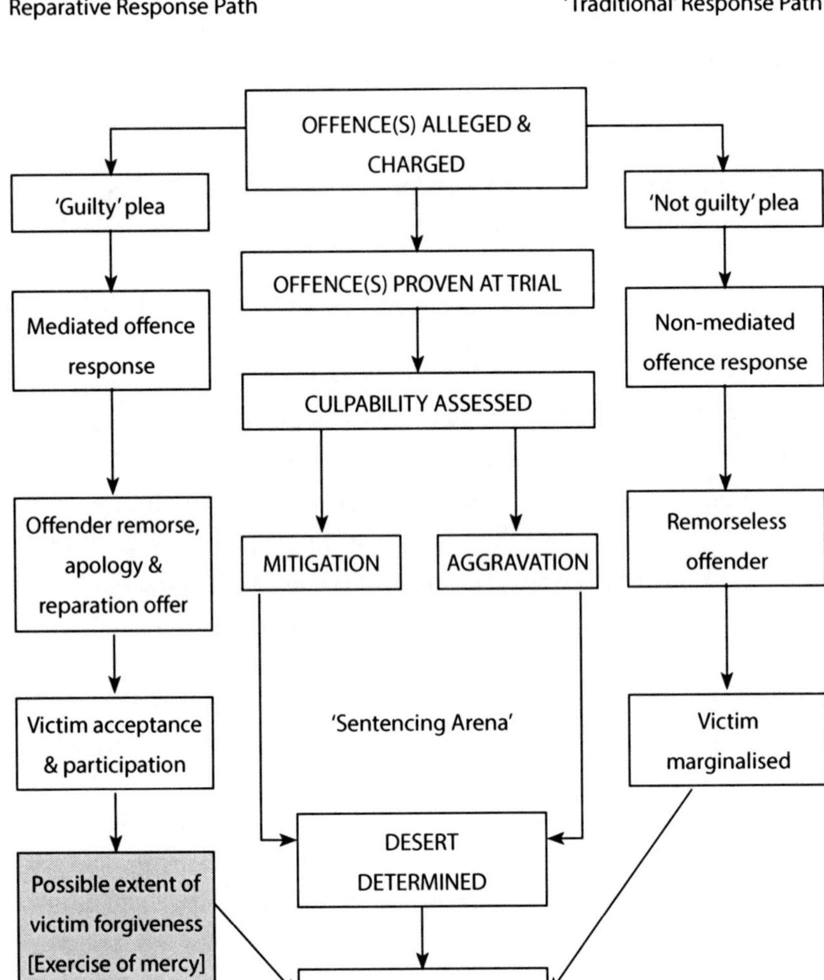

Figure 2: Criminal Justice Responses to Offenders and Offences

CHAPTER SEVEN

Exploring Victims' Rights

The Unique Status of Victims of Crime

As has become evident in the preceding chapter, much has been written about the supposed 'rights' of victims of crime in England and Wales in government publications dating back to the early-1990s, without assigning any substantive rights to them. Though the responsibilities of a number of government agencies and departments towards victims have been addressed in some considerable detail (Home Office, 2005a and 2005b *op. cit.*; Ministry of Justice, 2012f *op. cit.*), these provisions do not amount to the assignment of rights that are clearly identified and enforceable in law. The closest that any provision has come to conferring a right was the initiative taken by the Lord Chief Justice of England and Wales in his *Practice Direction* issued in 1990 on the matter of victim impact statements (4 All ER 640: III. 28 *op. cit.*).

Victims, as we have previously noted, are potentially uniquely placed within the criminal justice system to extend mercy and forgiveness to penitent offenders who are prepared to make amends for their crimes through apology, mediation and reparation. The restorative justice 'reparative model' outlined in *Chapter 6, supra* provides a means of enabling this to become a reality in deserving cases, and to a justifiable and reasonable extent. If this is a desirable state of affairs, then what is it that makes the assignment of rights to victims so problematic? For in *The Conquest of Granada*, the 17th-century poet John Dryden proposed: 'Forgiveness to the injured doth belong; for they ne'er pardon who have done the wrong.'[1] To understand this situation, it seems to be necessary to explore—albeit briefly—what rights are generally held to consist in, and the context in which the exercise of victim's rights would have effect if such were to be extended.

1. John Dryden (1631-1700), 'The Conquest of Granada', Part I. I. i, date unknown, quoted in *The Penguin Dictionary of Quotations*, Harmondsworth: Penguin Books, p.149 (1977 edition).

The Nature of Rights

Leif Wenar, prefaced his account of rights in the following terms:

> Rights are entitlements (not) to perform certain actions, or (not) to be in certain states; or entitlements that others (not) perform certain actions or (not) be in certain states.
>
> Rights dominate modern understandings of what actions are permissible and which institutions are just. Rights structure the form of governments, the content of laws, and the shape of morality as it is currently perceived. To accept a set of rights is to approve a distribution of freedom and authority, and so to endorse a certain view of what may, must, and must not be done. (Wenar, 2011: 1)

He further maintained that to understand and make sense of the many different forms of rights assertion it is necessary to categorise rights according to who is alleged to have them, what actions or states or objects the rights pertain to, why the right-holder (allegedly) has the right,[2] and how the asserted right can be affected by the right-holder's actions. Then, following the widely accepted Hohfeldian[3] protocol for the analysis of rights as to their form and function, he describes their basic components (known as the Hohfeldian 'incidents') that relate to the 'privilege', the 'claim', the 'power' and the 'immunity'. Moreover, since each of these 'incidents' or components has a distinctive logical form, they fit together in characteristic ways to create the structure of complex 'molecular' rights (Wenar, 2011*op. cit.*: 3).

Privilege-rights express what the right-holder has no duty not to do, and also what that person has permission to do in asserting their provisions. Some commentators such as Steiner (1994: 59-60) prefer the term 'liberties' to that of 'privileges', others give the terms different definitions (e.g. Thomson, 1990: 53-55),[4] but this need not detain us here. Claim-rights derive from an obligation or duty on the part of one person (or persons) to act in a certain way towards another as, for example, in the situation of an employer and an employee in which the former has a duty to pay the latter

2. Such is to say that *moral* rights are grounded in moral reasons, *legal* rights derive from the laws of the society, and *customary* rights exist by convention.
3. Named after Wesley Hohfeld (1879-1918), the American legal theorist who devised the analytical protocol described here (Hohfeld, 1919).
4. Both quoted in Wenar (2011 *op. cit.*) at p.4.

wages due to him or her for work performed in accordance with the terms of employment agreed between the two parties. However, claim-rights may extend to the duty of one or more persons not to act in a certain manner, as, for instance, in a person's claim-right that any person should not enter their property without permission or abuse their children. Privilege-rights and claim-rights are defined by Hart (1961) as 'primary' or 'first order rules' requiring that people perform or refrain from performing particular actions as duty-bearers in the circumstances concerned (Wenar, 2011 *op. cit.*: 5).

The 'secondary rules' identified by Hart and described by Wenar concern power-rights and immunity-rights which are somewhat more complex in conception. Power, in the Hohfeldian classification of 'incidents', enables the over-riding or modification of primary rules relating to one's own' incidents' or those of others. Thus a person has a power if, and only if, he or she has the ability within a set of rules to alter their own or another's Hohfeldian incidents. By way of example of this, a policeman has the power-right to instruct a driver to leave his vehicle (on suspicion of being intoxicated). This alters the normative situation of the driver by imposing a new duty upon him (to leave the vehicle), and so over-rides one of the driver's Hohfeldian privileges not to leave his vehicle. Similarly, in the example described earlier, the property owner who exercises his right to deny any or all persons access to his estate, but who invites his neighbour to enter, waives his right that the neighbour should not do so and thus alters his own Hohfeldian incident and claim-right. Ordering, promising, waiving, buying, selling or abandoning are means by which right-holders exercise a power to change their own Hofeldian incidents, or those of others.

Powers can, as Wenar points out, alter not only first order privileges and claims, but also second order ones as well. However, immunities (the fourth Hofeldian 'incident') occur when one person lacks the power to alter another's incidents—that other person thus having immunity from having his own incidents changed. By way of example here, if I lack the power to compel my neighbour not to access my property using a designated footpath that gives him a claim-right to do so, then he has immunity should he wish to exercise that right of access, however inconvenient his doing so may be to me. Put another way, my property-right does not in the given circumstances override his normative claim-right to use the footpath to cross the property.

Rights may, of course, be of an 'active' or 'passive' nature (Lyons, 1970), and these are also subsumed within the Hohfeldian 'incidents'. The privilege and the power are active rights that relate to the holder's own actions, whereas the claim and immunity rights are of a passive nature that regulate the actions of others. The policeman in the example given previously has an active privilege-right to patrol the highway to ensure that the traffic laws are complied with, and also an active power-right to order the apparently drunken driver to leave his vehicle. Similarly, a golfer playing in a tournament has a passive claim-right that other players not distract him when playing shots in his turn, and an employee has a passive immunity-right against unfair dismissal by an employer, i.e. that the employer does not so act.

There are, in life, many occasions on which rights appear to conflict, most commonly in the public rather than the private domain. Rights also compete for supremacy in certain circumstances, depending on the legal, moral or ethical stances invoked to maintain them. It is here that the test of 'reasonableness' has to be applied, and this is most frequently resolved by recourse to the legal framework of constitutional provisions. For instance, there is generally held within democracies to be a collective right to peaceful protest. How the term 'peaceful' is interpreted can become a matter of dispute, depending upon the situations of those involved (commonly the police and the public) in any particular set of circumstances. That the police have a duty to maintain order and public safety is normally accepted by law-abiding citizens as a necessary constraint upon the secular (such is to say group or private) interests of those wishing to protest. Thus on any given day the presence or manner of a protest, however peaceful, might be such as to pose a threat to public well-being which would conflict with the wider public interest of safety and security, and thus the duty of the police to maintain both. How such a situation is resolved will often depend upon the 'reasonableness' of the police behaviour in controlling it, and the 'reasonableness' of the protesters in accepting (or otherwise) the necessary limitations placed upon them not to act irresponsibly.

There is much more that might be said about 'rights', and indeed many volumes of scholarly literature on the subject bear witness to this fact. However, for our purposes within this work concerning the situation of victims of crime and their place within criminal justice, it becomes appropriate to return to that debate in the light of what has been considered here. The central issue that should concern us is whether, and to what extent, victims can be said to have 'rights', given the nature of the governmental provisions previously surveyed. If, however, such is not the case, then we need to discover how these rights can be justified and set in place.

Victims' Rights: A 'First Principle' Approach

Returning briefly to Hohfeld's analysis, it will be apparent that a distinction has to be made between 'positive' and 'negative' rights. For instance, Narveson (2001) suggests that the holder of a negative right is entitled to non-interference, while the holder of a positive right is entitled to provision of some good or service.[5] Further, according to Wenar (2011 *op. cit.*: 8), since both positive and negative rights are passive rights, some rights are neither negative nor positive. Privileges and powers cannot be negative rights, and privileges, powers and immunities cannot be positive rights. However, when it comes to the enforcement of rights, the differences disappear, and as Holmes and Sunstein (1999:43) insist, in the context of citizens' rights to state enforcement, all rights become positive.[6]

It is at this point that one encounters some profound differences of approach within the philosophical literature on rights, which become somewhat unhelpful for our purposes here.[7] Space in this work does not permit of a protracted discussion on this aspect, and neither do these differences move our argument in relation to victims' rights forward. The stance within this book is that victims are *owed* something as a result of their being offended against by those who cause them harm on the one hand, and on the other hand by the criminal justice system, the duty of which is to ensure that they are treated fairly and with due regard to the rules of natural justice.[8] In most jurisdictions in which criminal proceedings are conducted on a 'state *versus* defendant' basis it is implicit that the state subsumes the interests of all of

---

5. Quoted in Wenar (2011 *op. cit.*) at p.8.
6. Also quoted in Wenar (2011, *Ibid.*).
7. Such as the debate between Will and Interest theories of rights, the former propounded by Hart (1982 *op.cit.*), Wellman (1985) and Steiner (1994 *op. cit.*), and the latter by such as Bentham (1796), Lyons (1994), Kramer *et al.* (1998) and Kramer (2001).
8. A fundamental principle of which is that all parties to the proceedings should have the opportunity to be heard or be represented.

the other parties involved in the case, which must be taken to include both victims and witnesses.

The simple fact that victims have been offended against (to whatever extent) gives them a passive negative claim-right (that of not being abused or caused harm) against offenders whose duty it is not to cause such offence. This first-order claim-right extends logically to the expectation of apology and reparation (or compensation) from offenders or from the state, and, as parties to the offence(s) alleged, to have their personal circumstances given due consideration.

The situation of victims in relation to the state is, however, of a different nature. Here it must be held that since the state subsumes the interests of other parties (other than offenders) in criminal proceedings, it has a correlative duty to ensure that this responsibility is discharged fairly and justly in relation to all the parties concerned (including victims). It must, therefore, follow that in default of such duty, victims have a passive positive claim-right (that of being *owed* a duty by state)—positive (Cf. Holmes and Sunstein, 1999:43 *op. cit. supra*) due to the context of all citizens' rights to state enforcement being of a positive nature.

These situations change, however, in the event that offenders accept responsibility for the harm caused to victims, and are willing to make apology and reparation by way of mediation and commitment. In the event that the making of reparation becomes part of the mediation and sentencing outcome, and the victim accepts, in principle, the offer of reparation, it then becomes the duty of the offender to make it as owed to the victim. The reparation then becomes not only a first order passive claim-right,[9] but also effectively an active privilege-right which the victim as right-holder has no duty not to accept.

Having now established a measure of clarity as to the nature of rights, and in particular those putative rights of victims of crime, it becomes appropriate to examine the corollary responsibilities that flow logically from them. Though some writers have been critical of Hohfeld's analysis as

9. Because the reparation correlates to a duty on the part of the offender as the duty-bearer, and is owed to the right-holder (victim) for whom it also becomes the equivalent of a privilege-right over which he or she has a certain power to waive (in the mediation process), and immunity from others altering his or her claim to the reparation.

over-prescriptive and assertive (e.g. Glendon, 1991; O'Neill, 1996 and 2002), it has the merit of logical construction which has been helpful in this instance. It is, however, probably true to state that the 'rights talk' of recent years has focused much more on passive claim-rights and social expectations than on obligations and responsibilities.

Rights and Responsibilities

From the foregoing discussion it will now be evident that the state may be held to have certain defined duties (or responsibilities) within a 'rights-conscious' restorative and reparative model of criminal justice. These duties can be defined as follows:

- to include *within* criminal justice systems substantive arrangements for the reparation of victims of crime;
- to include within criminal justice processes procedures in which mediation between victims and remorseful offenders can lead to reparative outcomes and assist rational sentencing decisions;
- to extend to victims of crime (in addition to their status as potential witnesses) the status of 'stakeholders' within criminal justice processes;
- to include within sentencing practice sanctions that enable offenders to make due reparation to victims on either a custodial or non-custodial basis;
- to take due account prior to sentencing of the willingness (or otherwise) of offenders to take responsibility for their crimes, make apology, and reparation in full;
- to give victims within mediated outcomes the opportunity to extend forgiveness, and have such forgiveness reflected in sentencing decisions.

Each of the duties outlined above derives from the system of rights described previously, and none constitute assertions that are not correlative of those rights. However, setting such rights in place requires the state to accept responsibility for the legal and infrastructural changes to criminal justice practices that are implicit in their acceptance. Both politically and operationally such changes require a consensus to 'do justice better' than has been the case traditionally within predominantly retributive models of justice administration.

Such changes also have significant implications for offenders who have not, hitherto, been obliged to accept guilt, express remorse, or make apology and reparation to victims. Though compensation (or reparation) orders do exist in some jurisdictions however, in England and Wales these tend to be used *more* widely as alternatives to fines or other non-custodial penalties, and seldom as alternatives to a custodial sentence. The emphasis here is much more towards the avoidance of short-term custody combined with better treatment of victims of crime.

Victim Inclusiveness and Stakeholder Status

Victims 'empowered' by stakeholder status also have an important role to play within this improved form of justice. When they receive apology and the offer of reparation, many victims feel vindicated, that their personal harm is reduced, and also develop some understanding of the personal circumstances of the offenders who commit crime and those close to them. This, in turn, enables them to take a more charitable view of the offender, and not wish him or her to be subjected to excessive or unnecessarily severe punishment. But victims need an avenue to express these feelings without sentimentality, and, when they believe that it is merited, extend mercy through forgiveness which they wish those sentencing to take into account.

Inclusion of victims in this process need not extend to 'full-blown' allocution or a 'right' to participate directly in the sentencing process, but rather to an acknowledged status and the opportunity of making their views plainly heard either orally or in writing, and to have these views considered by the court in reaching its own decisions. But because victims have the claim-right identified in this work, it becomes the duty of the state to enable that right to be exercised. That is what stakeholder status is all about.

Offenders also, when accused of crime, have an established right to a fair hearing at which any remorse they may feel towards victims, and any willingness they may demonstrate to make amends through reparation have to be carefully weighed against the seriousness of the alleged offence(s), and therefore their culpability. Where victims, following upon a mediation process, express a wish that the offender be treated with leniency and thus extend mercy, research indicates that the likelihood of similar re-offending is significantly reduced. It is therefore in the overall interest of criminal justice that this two-way process should be a central feature of the adjudication of offences.

This chapter has been a necessary exploration into the nature of what might reasonably be claimed as the rights of victims within criminal justice. However, it is one thing to discern what rights may consist in, and quite another to ensure that such rights are given operational effect. In England and Wales, as in some other countries in Western Europe and elsewhere, there has been a traditional reluctance—due to a political and judicial preference for retributive justice dominated by 'just deserts' considerations—to empower victims adequately *within* the criminal justice process. This reluctance stems from two 'systemic' weaknesses or perceived vulnerabilities: the political 'fear' of being seen to be 'soft on crime', and the entrenched judicial 'resistance' to 'executive interference.' In *Chapter 8* which follows, the means by which these systemic weaknesses might be overcome becomes the focus of attention.

CHAPTER EIGHT

'Fault- Lines' and Fallacies

The Need to Re-Configure Criminal Justice

The experience of the past decades since the end of the Second World War within the criminal justice systems of many Western-style democracies should be sufficient to remind us that our philosophical and operational concepts of criminal justice are certainly questionable. What may have seemed appropriate two or three generations ago, and what we have inherited from those generations and perpetuated in terms of justice administration, is far from certainly 'fit for purpose' in the post-modern era. Our contemporary world has changed to an extent that would have been unimaginable to our forefathers, and yet our justice systems remain, in many respects, much as they bequeathed them to us.[1]

Within this chapter I shall venture to suggest that if criminal justice is to be made 'fit for purpose', a number of systemic weaknesses or 'fault-lines' have to be repaired or re-worked, and that a similar number of fallacies which have become perpetuated within contemporary penology have to be abandoned and consigned to the past. Indeed, until such a 'revisionist' agenda has been adopted and worked through, it is difficult to envisage how real and lasting progress can be made.

My colleague John Blad, writing in 2006, advanced the perceptive analogy that criminal justice seems, over recent years, 'to have come to resemble an old hospital that should have been demolished because it has collected so many viruses that it is, in fact, pathogenic' (Blad, 2006:135 *op. cit.*). However, as he further pointed out, when we demolish such a building because it is pathogenic, we transfer our patients to another place because we have not abandoned our desire to cure, but rather to enable us to get at the root cause of the problem. In the case of criminal justice, the root cause is not 'the desire

1. With the notable exception of the USA, most Western-style democracies have in the post-war era abandoned the use of the death penalty, and also forms of corporal punishment.

to do justice, but our misconceptions about, and misuse of punishment' (*Ibid*). The 'viruses' described by Blad precisely resemble the 'fault-lines' and fallacies that I wish briefly to describe here.

'Fault-lines' within Contemporary Criminal Justice Philosophy

The 'fault-lines' that require consideration here are broadly of two distinct categories: the one being political and strategic, and the other philosophical and procedural. However, as we shall shortly see, some of the 'fault-lines' veer closely towards the fallacies which are discussed subsequently, and indeed overlap with them in certain respects.

Crime Control or Crime Reduction

The first 'fault-line' concerns an apparent failure at the political level in England and Wales to be decide whether the primary purpose of the criminal justice system is crime *control* or crime *reduction*. This is a critical issue because there has been an evident tendency to use the two concepts within legislative conversations as though they are entirely interchangeable, and that the same policies fit either way or satisfy both aspirations. It is doubtful, since crime in endemic in every national situation, whether any country—even those with the most ruthless and draconian of punitive systems—has ever succeeded in *controlling* crime, since such would be an entirely pre-emptive endeavour and bound to fail.

Crime *reduction* on the other hand is an entirely different matter, requiring policies designed specifically to change behaviours by persuading offenders and assisting them to believe that a law-abiding lifestyle is preferable to one of crime. Neither retributive punishment alone, no matter to what extent apparently deserved, nor excessive use of imprisonment, evidently succeeds in securing such an objective. Crime reduction policies are, of course, an appropriate focus for criminal justice strategies, but to be deemed effective these strategies have to be designed to meet measurable outcomes in terms of reduced recidivism. Reparative and restorative models of criminal justice thus become evidently preferable to retributive ones in delivering effective justice.

Traditionalism

The second strategic 'fault-line' concerns the fact that within the Anglo-Saxon traditions of justice, retributive preferences for punishment have dominated the policy-making process over the past five decades for two very specific reasons. The first of these reasons is the 'stagnation' of policy initiatives due to predominantly bi-partisan political structures;[2] the second reason concerns the lack—since the demise successively of the 'rehabilitative' and 'justice' models of justice between the 1970s and early-1990s—of any alternative model of justice other than a return to retributive and deterrent concepts.

Such a situation makes it difficult for criminal justice to break free from 'retributive mode', and also stifles the development and acceptance of potentially ground-breaking concepts like that of restorative justice. The result is that reluctance to embrace the need for change consigns progressive initiatives to the margins of criminal justice practice to the extent that 'more of the same' becomes 'business as usual'. I return to this situation in later discussion of prevailing 'fallacies' within criminal justice thinking. Before passing on, however, there are two other aspects of this situation that deserve mention: one is the contemporary insistence in government circles on 'evidence-led' initiatives; the second is the extent to which media pressures and practices affect the thought processes and behaviour of politicians anxious to retain electoral credibility.

'Evidence-led' initiatives can only become a reality where there is a genuine desire to allow practice to be developed and tested free from pre-conception and prejudice. This evidently involves a measure of risk-taking and research funding which politicians and policy-makers are reluctant to entertain—particularly in an era of financial uncertainty. Media organizations with their own editorial styles and preferences are swift to criticise any form of initiative that could be claimed to be 'soft on crime', or which might appear to carry an element of 'public risk' either real or imagined. This plays into the hands of risk-averse politicians since it can become a justification

2. Such is to suggest that the domination of politics by only two effectively viable political parties leads to a convergence in policy considerations for electoral reasons. In two-party state situations lacking the innovative impetus of a substantial third party (or coalition of smaller but influential parties), neither of the main parties will wish to be seen to depart from the relatively 'safe' centre-ground of policy-making for fear of alienating party allegiances within the voting population or their own party organizations.

for avoidance and obfuscation which serves to increase policy stagnation.

Separation of Powers

The third 'fault-line' is a constitutional matter that derives from the 'separation' of the judiciary in England and Wales from the executive and legislative functions of government. Though there are historical reasons for this separation that were originally designed to preserve the integrity of judges and magistrates free from political interference and bias, judges in particular still retain a considerable discretion within trial and sentencing matters. Resort to sentencing guidelines in the past decade or so[3] has to some extent limited this discretion, though the relationship remains somewhat loosely defined.

Since judges in England and Wales are not civil servants as is the case in some European countries, and are appointed on the recommendation of the Judicial Appointments Commission to the Lord Chancellor,[4] the separation of powers concept is evidently not absolute. Rather more importantly, judges (and to a lesser extent magistrates) can frustrate the legislative provisions of parliamentary Acts by declining to use, or refraining from imposing certain forms of sentence, or by over-using others, when they see fit to do so.[5] [6]

---

3. With the establishment of the Sentencing Advisory Panel (SAP) under the Crime and Disorder Act 1998, and later the Sentencing Guidelines Council (SGC) under the Criminal Justice Act 2003 which superseded the SAP. The SGC is headed by the Lord Chief Justice, but reports annually to the Secretary of State for Justice who has no powers to direct its work or decisions other than in appointing an observer and forwarding proposals to it for consideration (Gibson, 2009 *op. cit.*:155).
4. Who is also the Secretary of State for Justice and a government appointee. The Lord Chief Justice chairs the Judicial Appointments Commission.
5. As they did in the 1980s and early-1990s in relation to extended sentences which were eventually discontinued and ultimately abolished in the Criminal Justice Act 1991. However, new provisions for these sentences were enacted in the Criminal Justice Act 2003 (section 226) for certain violent or sexual offences, and further modified in the Legal Aid, Sentencing and Punishment of Offenders Act 2012 (section 124).
6. As to over-use of sentences, the provisions for indeterminate sentences of imprisonment for public protection (ISPPs or IPPs) and extended sentences for public protection (ESPPs or EPPs) enacted in the Criminal Justice Act 2003 have resulted in many of those thus sentenced being detained in custody beyond their tariff dates (see: Gibson, 2009 *op. cit.*: 87; Prison Reform Trust, 2012a *op. cit.*:21). In March 2012, 6,017 persons were serving IPP sentences, 3,506 of whom were beyond their tariff dates. These provisions have, however, been modified in the Legal Aid, Sentencing and Punishment of Offenders Act 2012 which introduced new arrangements for extended determinate sentences (EDS).

The Uses of Imprisonment

The fourth 'fault-line' concerns the relationship between criminal justice legislation, the actual size and shape of the prison population in England and Wales, and the purposes of imprisonment itself. It seems scarcely believable that in 1948 the average daily prison population stood at 19,765, in 1968 it was 32,461, in 1988 reached 45,700, and in 2008 stood at 82,100. At the time of writing it exceeds 84,000 which reflects an imprisonment rate of 155 per hundred thousand of the population, compared with France with a similar population at 115 per 100,00, and Germany with 20 million more inhabitants at 83 per 100,000 (International Centre for Prison Studies, 2012). Moreover, in April 2012, 83 of the 134 prisons in England and Wales were officially overcrowded (Ministry of Justice, 2012c *op. cit.*).

Overcrowding in prisons is a major contributor to these places becoming (in John Blad's words) 'pathogenic' institutions, and this situation has been tolerated by successive governments for decades past. Worse still, it calls into question the fundamental purposes for which prisons were intended, and what such places are supposed to achieve on behalf of the public whom they serve. Legislation can be set in place to prohibit overcrowding (however defined), compel courts to limit the use of custody to those instances in which it is strictly unavoidable, or alternatively to authorise prisons to release those inmates closest to their release dates in order to create space for new arrivals who would exceed their certified capacity.

Various Western European nations have faced similar problems of excessive prison populations, and have resolved them by different legislative means (Cornwell, 2007 *op. cit.*: 165-6; 2009 *op. cit.*: 156 and *passim*).[7] It is, however, this particular fault-line that has contributed more than any other to the creation of a situation in which criminal justice has become confused as to its purposes, and significantly ineffective in delivering either crime control or crime reduction. Ultimately, the cause of this *malaise* is the 'policy-stagnation' outlined previously, and its outcomes in stifling correctional progress or reform over several decades. It has also had the unfortunate effect of 'marginalising' reparative and restorative justice from the mainstream of criminal justice.

7. Most notably Finland (see Lappi-Seppälä, 2001 and 2013), Germany (see Wiegend, 2001), The Netherlands (see Tak, 2001), Denmark (see Kyvsgaard, 2001), and Norway (see Larsson, 2001).

The Structure of Correctional Services

A fifth and unfortunate, though historical, fault-line within the criminal justice system of England and Wales in particular, lies in the failure–in spite of many attempts at reform[8]–to create a truly unified correctional services structure. The prison and probation services, with their very different forms of ethos and professionalism historically developed and at times somewhat jealously over-emphasised, deal with the same offenders at the different stages of the same sentence or court disposal. Probation officers are seconded to work within the casework structure of prison management, and in the event that in the future an expansion of community corrections were to be envisaged with lesser use of prison custody, the need for disciplined supervision of ex-prisoners making reparation within communities might suggest an expanded role for selected prison managers and officers on secondment to the Probation Service to enhance its effectiveness and public confidence.

Though such a future development is strictly tangential in relation to this work, it has some bearing on the development of a bifurcated system of criminal justice outlined in *Chapter 5, supra*, insofar as the need would inevitably arise for a much more integrated relationship between the two services than exists at the present time, and which might have some considerable 'political' appeal in fostering public and media confidence in an era of reduced dependence on the use of prison custody. However, as we shall see in the section that follows, the 'fault-lines' described briefly here are also to a considerable extent grounded in a number of fallacies that have inhabited criminal justice over recent decades, becoming the 'viruses' that have resulted in Blad's description of a pathogenic situation.

Fallacies within Contemporary Criminal Justice Philosophy

We must now examine five fallacies that are commonly encountered in relation to criminal justice and punishment philosophy, or which are issues of dispute that touch upon the exercise of mercy within criminal justice. Once again, volumes of literature have been written on these matters, with the result that the discussion must necessarily be confined in this work to issues

8. Including the formation of the Ministry of Justice in 2007 which assumed strategic responsibility for both the Prison and Probation Services within the National Offender Management Service (NOMS) previously established in 2004 (see Gibson, 2009 *op. cit.*: 115).

of principle, rather than expanded to reflect some of the wider concerns that might be claimed to afford alternative explanations.

Retribution versus Restoration

The fallacy that emerges from this debate is that of whether (or not) retribution and restoration are mutually exclusive agendas within criminal justice. We have laws (good, bad and indifferent in quality) to regulate social behaviour which would be entirely pointless without consequences (or sanctions) flowing from their infringement. This much stated, the wider issue is whether the purpose of these sanctions is merely to impose punishment, or to restore the damage to social relationships that offences cause. Is it more important to visit unpleasantness on those who do wrong than to seek ways to make good the harm done?

Our 'Anglo-Saxon attitudes' have traditionally steered us towards a primacy of retribution both historically and in the present era on the basis that it is the state's law that has been broken, and the state therefore has a duty to uphold the law and respond with just punishment to dissuade the offender from further offending, and others who might be tempted to act similarly from so doing. It is also asserted by those of a primarily retributive disposition that the punishment is deserved because the law has been broken, and that the punishment should involve unpleasantness in some approximate relationship to the seriousness of the offence.[9]

Proponents of a restorative ethic approach this situation from a different perspective, insisting that although the harm caused by offences has to be acknowledged, the *actual* damage is caused not merely to the law itself, but more to the social relationships that suffer disequilibrium as a result of them. Moreover, this disequilibrium affects all the parties involved in offences—victims, communities and offenders—rather than the law alone. Thus it becomes the responsibility of the offender to acknowledge the harm done, and make both apology and amends (through reparation) for it.[10]

---

9. Quite how this approximate relationship is achieved in practice is, of course, a matter of some debate, but in principle it is claimed that it is possible broadly to equate the nature and extent of the punitive 'unpleasantness' to that of the seriousness of the harm caused by the offence: the doctrine of proportionality.
10. Here, however it has to be acknowledged that in the earlier explanations of restorative justice by Howard Zehr (1990 *op. cit.*) and others, it was represented as the antithesis of retributive

Thus it may reasonably be concluded that the two approaches are not entirely irreconcilable or mutually exclusive since both acknowledge that consequences must result from offences, but it is the nature of, and motivations for the consequences that differ markedly. From a philosophical viewpoint, the greater question is that of which approach delivers the preferable and more equitable form of justice.

Mercy has no Place within Criminal Justice

Mercy is not a consideration for retributive justice based on desert because offenders must be punished in relation to their culpability and in proportion to the harm caused by their offences. They must also be punished to deter them from further offending, and by way of example to others who might offend similarly. Thus because punishment is a deserved response to crime, the state (represented by those responsible for sentencing) has no responsibility or capacity to extend mercy, even though it does have a duty to consider issues of mitigation in the process of imposing punishment. Mitigation and mercy are, therefore, neither inter-changeable nor relative within an entirely retributive concept of criminal law.

Mercy becomes a possibility within a restorative ethic which perceives victims rather than the state as the entity more harmed by offences. This is, as we have noted earlier (in *Chapter 6*), because victims are uniquely placed to extend mercy and should have a right to do so within the justice process should they wish. However, it has also been pointed out (see *Chapter 3*) that within the literature on legal philosophy there is a divergence of views on the place of mercy within criminal and civil law, as evidenced by the writings of Twambly (1985 *op. cit.*), Tasioulas (2003 *op. cit.*), Lauchs (2005 *op. cit.*) and others. It is further of interest that Twambly and Tasioulas appear to disagree about the place of mercy within civil law—a conflict of opinions that does not necessarily negate the potential for mercy to be shown within a restorative concept or philosophy of justice.[11] This divergence of views will be further examined in *Chapter 9*, but it is maintained here that

justice. This position was later modified by Zehr (and Mika, 1998 *op. cit.*; Zehr, 2002 *op. cit.*).

11. It should be noted here that Tasioulas evidently perceives mercy within the criminal law as being tied to the punishment process, and thus it enters the province of sentencing and becomes the potential responsibility of judges and other similar officials to extend. For reasons already explained within this work, such a view is not endorsed in this analysis.

it is, nonetheless, a fallacy that mercy has no place within criminal justice.

Bifurcated Justice as Injustice

The third fallacy concerns the morality (or otherwise) of criminal justice systems designed to deal differently with genuinely remorseful and intransigent or remorseless offenders respectively. Such an approach is entirely different from that of the 'twin-track' sentencing policies that emerged in England and Wales during the 1990s with the resurgence of 'law and order' punitivism which insisted that serious offenders should be dealt with more harshly, and less serious offenders more leniently through 'punishment in the community' (here see, in particular, Cavadino and Dignan, 1997 *op. cit.,passim*; Bottoms, 1977, 1980: 1-24).

The 'punitive bifurcation' described above is, of course, liable to charges of injustice, seeking as it did to single out certain specific forms of (violent and sexual) offending for exemplary punishment over and above that strictly deserved. Equally, the leniency extended towards less serious offenders (dubbed 'punishment in the community') was a cynical political move to limit the growth of the prison population while still being seen to be 'tough on crime'.

The form of bifurcation advanced here is of an entirely different motivation. It seeks to afford opportunities for offenders to accept responsibility for their offences, make apology and offer reparation to those harmed, and 'earn back' their status as citizens through restoration. Reparation can be made either in custody or in the community, or in some sentence formats both,[12] maintaining the principles of desert and parsimony.[13] On the other hand, since there is no necessary expectation that offenders should show remorse and take responsibility, the 'traditional' mode of sentencing and sanctions would remain in place to deal with them justly, yet less leniently, and strictly

12. Such, for instance as a 'hybrid' custodial sentence where unavoidable, but with a specified minimum term to be spent in prison custody combined with a similar period spent working in the community to make reparation thereafter. The overall sentence period would reflect the seriousness of the offence in terms of desert, while the custodial term would be strictly limited to a maximum of one third of the total sentence period to comply with the principle of exercising parsimony in the deprivation of liberty.
13. The principle of parsimony dictates that punishment should be reduced to the minimum extent consistent with marking the gravity of offences, excluding other additional considerations such as that of general deterrence of others who might be tempted to offend similarly.

in terms of desert. In the case of the former, and where reparation is agreed by mediation between victims and offenders prior to the sentencing stage, the opportunity would arise for victims to express a disposition towards mercy, and request that the court reflect this in sentencing decisions.

The form of bifurcation proposed here suggests a more appropriate form of justice in a contemporary setting than the manifestly unjust mode in which it was conceived in the 1990s, and justifiably criticised. It overturns the objection (or fallacy) that bifurcation in penal policies is inherently unjust, while at the same time envisioning a system of justice that empowers and vindicates victims by extending to them a form of rights suggested in *Chapter 7*, previously. It would additionally hold out to offenders a substantive means of making amends for their wrongdoing, and the probability that re-offending would also be reduced in the longer term.

Reduced Use of Imprisonment Increases Public Risk

In spite of many hours spent searching criminological references and internet sources, it has proved impossible to discover any reliable or authoritative studies that have attempted to quantify this assertion so frequently advanced by the media and other 'law and order' proponents in a Western European context. This is scarcely surprising since a correlation between reduced use of custody and consequently increased crime rates would be difficult to establish with any confidence on the one hand, and on the other hand, incidences of imprisonment reduction over recent decades have been relatively rare occurrences, the outcomes of which might take months or even years to become evident even if reliable data could be gathered.

It would seem altogether likely that deliberate policies to reduce the use of imprisonment would select the shorter sentenced sector of prison populations within which crime is of lesser seriousness for implementation. Moreover, since such prisoners spend relatively short periods in custody before release back into communities, and generally present a lower risk to public safety than do more serious offenders, any re-offending that they might commit would be likely to attract relatively meagre public or media attention.

What is, however, evident is that the highest re-conviction rates within 12 months of release from custody lie within the short (12 months or less) sentence range of which only one half of the sentence period is spent in custody, and the remainder at present unsupervised within the community (Ministry of Justice, 2012g). The short periods spent in custody largely preclude such prisoners receiving any substantial assistance to reduce recidivism, and the fact that they return to their communities relatively unsupervised therefore places them 'at risk' of further offending.

All things considered, the assertion that lesser use of imprisonment increases public risk may appeal to intuition but it is unsustainable: more to the point is the probability that if short prison sentences were to be replaced by effectively supervised community sentences, both recidivism and actual public risk might be significantly reduced.[14]

A Political and Social Consensus for Penal Reform is Impossible to Achieve

This fifth and final 'fallacy' has to be dismantled since quite simply it is factually untrue. The Finnish experience of the 1970s and onwards into this new millennium, and those also of its neighbouring Nordic nations (Lappi-Seppälä, 2013 *op. cit.*), provide abundant evidence that where there is a political will and determined leadership to embark on radical penal reform, significant and durable change can be achieved and maintained.

A consensus to implement penal reform requires the political leadership to insist that reform is necessary for soundly based criminological and economic reasons, that it is going to happen, and that therefore the debate is about *how* this will be done rather than *whether* it can be achieved. In the Finnish experience, this required an alliance of politicians, social policy-makers, academics, criminal justice practitioners,[15] the judiciary and the media committed to determining the extent of reform necessary, and how it would be implemented. However, one of the enduring characteristics of the Nordic nations is their democratic tradition of valuing social equality and welfare distribution[16] to a considerably greater extent than is evident in the wide disparities of income and wealth within Britain and some other

14. Particularly in view of the fact that Ministry of Justice statistics confirm that court ordered community sentences are eight percentage points more effective than short (less than 12 months) custodial sentences in reducing recidivism (Ministry of Justice, 2010 *op.cit.*).
15. Including the police, prison, probation and prosecution services, and those responsible for the supervision and operation of mediation services and community sanctions.
16. Most notably in health, educational, social welfare and community-focused services available and accessible to all citizens irrespective of social status, gender or ethnicity.

Western European nations.

The social cohesiveness of Finnish society and concern for the quality of life of all its members undoubtedly aided the consensus that reform was not only necessary but also economically unavoidable. It was achieved with a massive reduction in the use of prison custody from around 180 per hundred thousand of the population in the early-1960s to a sustained rate of some 65 per hundred thousand from the 1980s and onwards, and without a significant increase in the rates of overall crime.

This chapter has highlighted a range of important issues that bear upon impediments in the path of doing justice in a more enlightened and considerate manner than has been characteristic of the British tradition hitherto. It also points towards a more inclusive and potentially merciful form of justice with a wider stake-holding than that merely of the state and offenders. Perhaps, as we shall explore in *Chapter 9*, it also opens the way to defining a substantive reparative and restorative philosophy of corrections that has allegedly defied a complete consensus among its adherents during years past.

CHAPTER NINE

Mercy and Restorative Justice

The purpose of this short book has been to explore the concept of mercy within criminal justice in a general sense, but more specifically in its place within a reparative and restorative context of justice administration. Such a journey became necessary because the existing literature on the virtue of mercy is perplexing, frequently confused with mitigation, and largely pre-supposes the inevitability of predominantly retributive punishment. As we have seen in earlier chapters, there are those who believe that mercy has no place within criminal justice: a belief which I have suggested is erroneous, and the reasons for this have been explained.

Ultimately, the capacity to extend mercy resides not with judges or other state officials[1], but with those offended against who suffer the harm occasioned by wrongdoing. It is only they who can extend forgiveness, and it should be their right to do so should they feel so disposed. Recalling the case of Abdelbaset Ali al-Megrahi described in *Chapter 2*, we may see with hindsight that if the decision to release him was ultimately based upon widely emerging doubt as to the safety of his conviction—even among some of the victims—then it was one of justice and not of mercy, his medical condition notwithstanding. In the event his sentence was effectively quashed (or set aside) rather than commuted.[2]

1. Such for instance as Parole Boards or similar bodies whose actions are circumscribed by procedural rules and operational limitations. The exercise of the Royal Prerogative of Mercy in Britain is an executive function of government delegated to Justice Ministers on behalf of the Crown, and therefore answerable to parliament. Though it may be used in exceptional circumstances to mitigate the extent or severity of sentencing decisions or their effect, and even be perceived as having a 'merciful' motivation, it remains a political decision related to expediency rather than mercy.
2. If, however, the sentence was 'set aside' for other underlying reasons not disclosed within the decision to release al-Megrahi on compassionate grounds, then the decision was of an entirely political nature bearing on neither justice nor mercy. If effectively quashed due to doubts as to its safety, then it was undeserved because the extent of his culpability could not be ascertained, and thus the objection in principle advanced by Professor Ross becomes unsustainable.

It has frequently been asserted that one of the main shortcomings of restorative justice as it has developed over the years since Eglash, Zehr and others first gave it expression (see *Chapter 1, supra*) is that it lacks a unified philosophy to which all its adherents can subscribe. Such a criticism is not without some foundation for reasons that we should now examine with a view to considering how this situation might be resolved. Further, if mercy is to occupy a central place within criminal justice both in theory and in practice, and particularly within a restorative philosophy of justice, then its claim for such status has to be substantiated because otherwise it will remain a 'virtue' but nothing more.

Why Restorative Justice Remains Problematic

In this new millennium there is a clearly evident need for a re-thinking of the purposes of criminal justice, since the traditional reliance on retributive and deterrent policies has failed significantly to achieve crime reduction and decrease rates of recidivism. That is the evidence of 'what doesn't work', and fails at unaffordable cost in both fiscal and human terms. Restorative justice has offered one route towards a significant change in criminological thinking which could accommodate, to some extent, both the 'exclusive traditional' approach and also a more inclusive reparative ethic, giving victims of crime an appropriate stakeholding within justice systems.

For as we have seen in earlier chapters, retributive and restorative agendas are not necessarily mutually exclusive or ultimately conflicting, the latter accepting that there have to be consequences when offending occurs, but rather calling for a more considered and constructive approach towards the resolution and outcomes of criminal wrongdoing. Whether or not this implies a 'paradigm revolution' or a 'paradigm shift' becomes the moot point at issue. It is in this particular area of considerations that restorative justice has exposed its own 'fault-lines' in former years: a situation that has not been entirely repaired and leaves it still open to justifiable criticism.

The first restorative justice 'fault-line' is the fact that as a predominantly 'practitioner-inspired' movement for change, and in spite of having clearly expressed differences of principle with traditional justice (Cf. Eglash, Zehr and others *supra*), it had evident 'abolitionist' roots which set it in a somewhat antagonistic framework in relation to justice systems struggling to maintain a socially coherent ethos in the wake of the demise of the rehabilitative and justice-model prescriptions of the post-conflict era. This was an unfortunate, even if unintended, negative consequence of the early conceptions of restorative justice (Umbreit *et al.*, 2005 *op. cit.*: 302-4).

Moreover, the concept of restorative justice was adopted and expressed in the environments of many different countries in which practices of resolving the conflicts of crime through mediation and social healing were already deeply embedded in the cultures of 'first-nation' peoples.[3] It was, therefore, scarcely surprising that differences of interpretation and implementation of its principles assumed a territorial orientation that had resonance for the cultures concerned. With hindsight this diversity may be seen as a strength rather than as weakness of restorative justice, although it became a matter of criticism for its apparent lack of philosophical 'standardisation' by those who perceived it as a threat to the prevailing retributive agendas of Western European nations in particular.

To complicate matters further, there arose within Western Europe in particular a divergence of views between those (predominantly academic) protagonists of restorative justice who perceived it in 'absolutist' terms as a means of paradigm-*change*, and those of a more 'incrementalist' persuasion (predominantly practitioners) who saw it as a means of achieving a longer-term paradigm-*shift*. The former evidently wanted restorative justice to be *the* criminal justice system of choice in place of retributively focused agendas, while the latter were more inclined towards a progressive or stepwise approach to incorporate restorative practices increasingly within existing criminal justice systems. This situation subsequently became the second 'fault-line' within the restorative justice movement, and has yet to be entirely resolved.

In addition, at the pragmatic level of restorative justice practice, and in an 'evidence-led' era of penal policy-making constrained by economic uncertainty, it became evident that reparative and restorative initiatives would face problems of opportunity and in securing resource funding, and

3. Most notably in Northern America, Australia, New Zealand, Africa and parts of the Middle-East, many of which areas had been colonised by Western European nations in subsequent generations, and whose legal systems were governed by Western concepts of justice administration.

thus the risk of becoming marginalised and unable to assemble a core of disciplined research evidence to support the claim to have the potential to reduce recidivism. This led to a serious consideration of practicalities and even of priorities, and as a result, to the emergence of a third 'fault-line' (see, for instance, Zehr and Toews, 2004; Sharpe, 2004; Umbreit *et al.*, 2005 *op. cit.*: 303).[4]

These difficulties apart, there remained the long shadow cast by traditional justice systems, supporters of which could somewhat perversely continue to claim that the more 'merciful' instincts of restorative justice, largely untried and untested, amounted to little more than an agenda for being 'soft on crime' and on offenders. In such a situation, the restorative movement continued to be perceived as 'problematic', and could therefore safely be confined to the margins of criminal justice practice.

Is a 'Core Philosophy' of Restorative Justice Essential?

The foregoing discussion has highlighted a number of the perceived difficulties that the restorative justice movement has faced, particularly over the two most recent decades. It is, however, a movement which has expanded on a worldwide basis, and which has established at least a foothold within many national criminal justice systems. That it alone, of all other prescriptions for administering justice, entails a clearly visible inclusive and merciful component makes it an antidote to repressive and exclusive punitive processes.

Since restorative approaches to justice have an ancient lineage in many countries including Britain, and these pre-date the retributive (and other) motivations of later centuries as we have seen in *Chapter 1*, *supra*, it might be argued that restorative justice has established its credentials in no uncertain manner. Reparation has always existed as a core ingredient of its practices, and this alone implies that victims of crime have a long-established right to consideration and participation in justice. That this right was diminished by the greediness of monarchs and feudal lords seeking to make criminal justice a revenue-earning concern and the basis of social control in no sense dilutes

4. This 'fault-line' as Susan Sharpe (2004) pointed out, separated those of a 'purist' persuasion who wished to strictly limit the extent of the restorative justice movement to focus it on core issues and practices, and those of a 'maximalist' preference for widening its scope to the extent that it might become so diffuse that it would be hard to distinguish what made its policies and practices uniquely restorative.

this historical legacy or its legitimacy (Cornwell, 2012: 78-9).

This much having been stated, the 'fault-lines' and fallacies of contemporary criminal justice described in the previous chapter, and the 'fault-lines' of the restorative justice movement discussed earlier in this chapter, clearly show the need for an extent of re-definition—even, possibly, to the extent of re-defining the essential nature of mercy within criminal justice itself. In the concluding section of this chapter I shall attempt this somewhat daunting task.

Before doing so, however, there are a few necessary observations (or pre-conditions) that have to be suggested. First, a core belief in the essential 'rightness' of retribution as a response to, and consequence of crime is unassailable for as long as it remains un-vindictive and ultimately constructive rather than destructive. Second, a similarly core belief in the place of mercy within criminal justice does not annul the necessity for a reciprocal response to offending, but insists that the response is inclusive of the circumstances and of the willingness of victims to extend forgiveness to those who cause them harm. The third pre-condition supposes willingness among all those working to promote reparative and restorative outcomes of criminal justice to re-consider 'absolutist' and 'incrementalist' preferences, in the interests of finding sufficient common ground to allow the movement to move into the future with a unified confidence.

Is There a Need to Re-evaluate Restorative Justice and Mercy?

Societies world-wide alter in their structure over time in accordance with the changing circumstances and patterns of economic and demographic development within them. Many nations have witnessed a marked demise of rural communities as urbanisation has increased, and with this trend a fracturing of the traditional social relationships and values that formerly bound families and neighbourhoods together in common cause and interests. This development has also changed the extent to which the patterns of guidance and rule-conforming training, formerly provided or exercised by respected older generation family and community members, is able to influence the lives of younger people. New urban communities, however desirable for economic reasons, now frequently lack the earlier sense of social cohesion and citizenship responsibilities more evident in bygone times.

These forms of social change have also encouraged the tendency for populations to congregate on the basis of ethnicity, religious belief or relative affluence, thus stressing rather than reducing differences of socialisation and behavioural preference, and increasing feelings of communal isolation and *anomie*. These are also the conditions in which crime tends to increase and social intolerance becomes more widespread. Such developments are, of course, also the by-products of apparent social progress as living standards have also largely improved universally, and yet differences of relative affluence, opportunity and social status have become more marked.

A typical instance of this social transformation has occurred in Southern Africa over recent years, made the more difficult by incoming migrations of populations as refugees from states still in the aftermath of de-colonisation (Mbambo and Skelton, 2003:272-8). It has resulted in a marked diminution in the African value of *ubuntu*,[5] or what we in Western cultures might term communitarian relationships of tolerance, generosity of spirit, and of goodwill. It remains, however, a curious paradox that in many respects where sub-populations congregate along ethnic, religious or other lines, they frequently do so to regain and preserve a traditional sense of belonging akin to *ubuntu* which becomes strong *within* these communities, but which can also be perceived as introspective and exclusive by those of other social identity.

There is no doubt that the spirit of forgiveness has heavily characterised the South African interpretation of *ubuntu* both nationally in the work of the Truth and Reconciliation Commission set up following the end of the *apartheid* era, and more locally within provincial government practices and legislation. This was undoubtedly due to the inspired leadership and example of the late President Nelson Mandela and Archbishop Desmond Tutu, and of others who had suffered so grievously under the former regime during the *apartheid* years.

Forgiveness and willingness to reconcile are hallmarks of the spirit of generosity and compassion which only those harmed or wronged are in a

---

5. *Ubuntu* is both a guide to social conduct and a philosophy of life as an African worldview. As Archbishop Desmond Tutu explains, it is difficult to translate into Western language. 'It speaks of the very essence of being human .. [meaning that people] are generous, hospitable, friendly, caring and compassionate. They share what they have... We say "a person is a person through other people." *Ubuntu* is linked to forgiveness which gives people resilience, enabling them to survive and emerge still human despite all efforts to dehumanise them' (Tutu, 1999).

position to extend. These virtues combine to result in merciful behaviour towards those who are guilty of the wrongdoing, but are equally contingent upon the genuine expression of remorse and apology by those who offend. The larger question then becomes that of why, if these virtues are of the essence of social justice, we cannot interpret and include them within the core practices of criminal justice.

This question brings us to the brink of the decision-making problems that lie at the heart of 'doing justice better'. For it remains an evident truth that retributive justice is essentially a repressive form of justice designed to suppress crime and thus also those who commit it. It is also, stripped of other supposed justifications, an exclusive form of human behaviour that, through insistence upon the necessity for the use of retrospective punishment, deliberately alienates offenders from their communities. In so doing, it also marks them out as 'bad' people, and significantly inhibits their chances of effective social re-integration.

Reparative justice works towards entirely different outcomes of the justice process. It seeks to provide the opportunity for genuine repentance, the making good of harm done, the recognition of those harmed, and an earned route towards deserved social restoration. Such a form of justice dignifies the status of those offended against with the potential to express forgiveness, and provides, through their right to extend mercy, an inclusive potential for social re-integration.

In former work I have likened retributive justice to a thinly veiled form of 'social outlawry' (Cornwell, 2012 *op. cit.*:84-5), and see no good reason to recant from this view. For while it may lay a claim to promote responses to crime grounded in desert and proportionality, its outcomes in terms of collateral and life-limiting damage to offenders and their dependants become issues largely beyond the considerations of the law. Many offenders are already casualties of social disadvantage and other deficits prior to offending, and while these symptoms may not excuse their wrongdoing, they evidently require assistance rather more than censure which consequentially becomes ultimately disproportionate. On the other hand, reparative justice should be as applicable to offenders as to victims, seeking to redress these deficits and provide within its processes the means by which they can be assisted to lead law-abiding lives in the future. If the central purpose of criminal justice is to achieve crime reduction, then this becomes an imperative that cannot be ignored.

The question posed in the heading of this section suggests a crucial issue within contemporary criminal justice that has to be resolved. Restorative justice, as we have seen, has its own 'fault-lines' which at present contribute towards its marginalisation within justice systems, and confine it to (at best) considerations of less serious and predominantly youthful offending. Its prescriptions also amount to a daunting proposition for politicians because a 'paradigm-shift' in the form and extent it implies call for great political courage and leadership to enable their implementation. The prescriptions are also a 'gift' to leaders of parliamentary oppositions who may, quite unjustifiably, capitalise upon them as being 'soft on crime'.

Though the piecemeal and culturally dispersed nature of the development of restorative justice practices may, in fact, be claimed to be advantageous, the structural need for professionally trained and accredited mediation practitioners becomes an essential component if implementation is to be effective (e.g. Anderson, 2013: 479-499 *passim*). The linkage between these practitioners, victim services, prosecutors and the courts has also to be formalised within criminal law.

Whether or not a social consensus can be achieved to enable the transformation of restorative justice into a mainstream preference for 'better justice' will hinge upon the quality and determination of political leadership on the one hand, and upon the willingness of the participants (academics, judiciary, legal professionals, criminal justice practitioners and the media) to set aside pre-dispositions to impede or obstruct such progress from a 'traditionalist' perspective. However, the example of the Finnish experience (Lappi-Seppälä, 2013 *op. cit.*) serves to confirm that such a consensus is achievable.

This leaves the restorative justice movement itself to resolve its internal 'absolutist *versus* 'incrementalist' dichotomy in the interests of its own salvation. This may mean restricting the size of the 'restorative justice tent' (Cf. Sharpe, 2004 *supra*) to a binding statement of core values and approved processes to which all of its proponents can and must subscribe. The need for such a consensus is, however, a critical pre-condition for its own future credibility.

Towards a Re-definition of Mercy

And finally, Mercy within the context of criminal justice has to be re-defined beyond the status of a 'virtue' to that of a philosophical and operational component of true justice. This means that there has to be clarity as to its rightful place within justice processes, whose prerogative it is to extend it, and a clear distinction drawn between this and the exercise of other forms of mitigation, leniency and compassion which remain matters of judicial (and in certain instances executive) interpretation. Recalling the *al-Megrahi case* discussed at some length in *Chapter* 2, *supra*, the executive decision to release him on 'compassionate' grounds involved legal and procedural implications far beyond the appropriateness of the decision in the circumstances. Essentially, it implied that an executive power which lay beyond the law had been legally regulated, and a new precedent possibly thereby created (Farmer, 2009 *op. cit.*: 2).

There are two points within a restorative concept of justice at which it may be claimed that opportunities for victims to extend forgiveness and mercy could be accommodated. The first occurs at the stage at which an offence has been discovered and the alleged offender (and victim(s)) identified. In the event that the offender acknowledges responsibility and is prepared to offer apology and reparation, the case becomes open to mediation to arrive at a resolution acceptable to both parties before a decision over prosecution is made. As an outcome of the mediation process the victim may decide to extend a measure of forgiveness and request that the offender should be dealt with more leniently than might otherwise seem deserved, or even not prosecuted, in view of the agreement to make reparation, and acceptance of his apology as sincerely made.

The second point might be reached when a decision to prosecute the offender has been made in view of the seriousness of the offence and notwithstanding any mediated outcome that might be reached in advance of the case coming to trial. Once a finding of guilt has been reached and the conviction recorded, the process of determining an appropriate sentence ensues, and aspects of mitigation and aggravation are considered. At this stage also, it would be incumbent on the court to consider any victim impact (or personal) statement submitted to it, and take due note of any wish the victim might express in relation to forgiveness and/or willingness to extend mercy and accept reparation. Such sentiments might otherwise have been expressed in the event that the victim had given evidence as a witness prior to the finding of guilt and conviction having been made.

Either way, the place of mercy within the criminal justice process would have become 'institutionalised' to an acceptable extent that kept it separated from considerations of mitigation which have proved problematic and confusing in much of the literature hitherto (Cf. Smart, 1968 *op. cit.* and others). Thus we might re-define mercy within criminal justice as 'the expressed wish of a person wronged by crime to extend a measure of forgiveness towards an offender, and request that any punishment imposed be moderated to reflect the victim's desire for parsimony to be exercised.'

Definition of mercy in this manner would have the merit of not interfering with the principle of just desert which would, in any event, remain a primary consideration for those entrusted with sentencing. Thus, also, sentencing decisions would effectively balance desert of punishment against desert of mercy, the concept of which was previously introduced and discussed in *Chapter 4, supra.*

In the final chapter that follows, I shall attempt to draw together all the main strands of discussion in those preceding it which bear upon the context in which mercy might appropriately be afforded an institutionalised status within restorative criminal justice systems of the future.[6]

6. Here it should be noted once again that the concept of reparative and restorative justice advanced in this work in no sense negates the need for 'traditional' processes to be retained as a means of dealing justly with offenders who deny responsibility for their offences, or remain remorseless towards those harmed by their criminal actions or neglect.

CHAPTER TEN

In Conclusion

On a Sad Note

As this final chapter is written the world mourns the passing of Nelson Mandela at the age of 95 years in Johannesburg, Republic of South Africa, of which nation he became the first democratically elected black African Head of State. Lawyer, anti-*apartheid* activist, prisoner, statesman, Nobel Peace Laureate and President, his courage, endurance, dignity, humility and devotion to forgiveness and reconciliation became the abiding memories of his remarkable life. Born a *Xhosan*, he became known as 'Madiba' or 'Tata', and was universally respected and even revered as the 'Father of the Rainbow Nation' as he termed the emergent post-*apartheid* South Africa. Honoured by many nations across the world, it is difficult to conceive of any human being who more exemplified the virtues of mercy, forgiveness and reconciliation that lie at the core of this book which is most respectfully dedicated to his memory.

Within this Book

This work was inspired by the failing state of criminal justice in Britain, as in many other contemporary democracies, particularly during the past two decades. The reasons for this situation lie in a number of factors which may, at root, be summarised as political 'stagnation', confused purposes, traditional obstinacy, and fear of reform that might necessitate a modification of the primacy of retributive punishment. Public attitudes towards crime and punishment are more a matter of supposition than of accurate determination, but are also evidently influenced to a considerable extent by an incessant focus upon serious crime in the mass media, generative of a 'fear of victimisation' markedly disproportionate to its actual occurrence within the daily lives of most citizens.

The results of this situation become self-perpetuating and cyclic: supposed public fear inspired by media sensationalism feeds punitive dispositions towards offenders; 'populist punitiveness'[1] induces policy-making paralysis within governments; and this paralysis encourages politicians to adopt increasingly punitive legislative attitudes and measures for fear of being perceived as 'soft on crime'. Increasingly punitive measures obviate the exploration of alternative crime reduction strategies and also inflate prison populations. And high rates of post-custodial recidivism complete the cycle by increasing public anxiety.

To understand how this state of affairs came to exist, it has been necessary to trace the ways in which criminal justice has changed over the centuries since nation states became a reality in the Middle-Ages in Britain and more widely within Western Europe. Account also had to be taken of the 'colonial legacies' that dominated justice systems within many other emerging and now independent nations across the world today. But this book also had a more precise focus in a perception that the processes and practices of criminal justice as these have developed in the post-modern era lacked an essential dimension or ingredient, and that this ingredient lay within the concept of mercy.

The advent of restorative justice from the late 1970s and onwards exemplifies the age-old traditions of reparative community justice that pre-dated the emergence of nation states, and yet which still exist among first nation populations in many areas of the modern world. That these traditions were more 'merciful' in a strictly definitional sense of the term, and gave due consideration to victims of crime and the responsibilities of offenders, provided the basis for a re-conceptualisation of contemporary justice and its evident shortcomings.

The fact that restorative justice has yet to establish itself within mainstream criminal justice in a fully-fledged and acknowledged sense has many causes and impediments which have been revealed in this work. Dominant among these impediments have proved to be traditionalism, political 'stagnation' and inertia, the deeply-rooted retributive instinct within punitive justice itself, the impact of media sensationalism of crime, and the persistent over-use of

1. A term originally described by Anthony Bottoms (1995) and subsequently developed by David Garland (2002 *op. cit.*) in terms of a 'post-modernist angst' or fear of crime within populations which is highly questionable (see also: Tonry (2003) *op. cit.*:4).

prison custody as a means of alleviating the widely exaggerated or supposed public 'fear of crime and victimisation'.

The development of restorative justice as a predominantly 'practitioner-led' search for better justice has also had its own apparent impediments which have been acknowledged in this work. Foremost among these have been its piecemeal adoption and adaptation world-wide as responses to the culturally different traditions of justice in the countries that have espoused it, and despite the fact that its original formulation and values were clearly expressed. It has also to an extent been hampered by a divergence of views and agendas within its own movement between those of a somewhat 'absolutist' approach seeking its adoption as a replacement for existing criminal justice systems, and others of a more 'incrementalist' persuasion who perceive it as a developmental and progressive means of ameliorating the evident shortcomings of existing processes by working within and alongside them.

The chapters of this book have been inter-twined by four central themes or contentions: that the concept of mercy has been widely misunderstood and confused with that of mitigation; that mercy is the province of those alone who become victims of crime to extend; that victims of crime deserve greater recognition and status within criminal justice; and that a restorative philosophy of justice has the potential to transcend the retributive instincts of the past, and deliver a more considerate and effective justice for the future. To this end, the work has been devoted to the formulation of what is, in effect, a restorative philosophy of justice based on widely acknowledged foundational principles, but capable of being implemented in a practical manner in pursuit of better justice.

It remains evident, however, that achievement of such ambitions for better justice inevitably requires a 'paradigm-shift' of considerable proportion, based upon a social consensus that significant change is essential in order to make many criminal justice systems in contemporary democracies 'fit for purpose'. Such change requires inspired political leadership and a willingness to acknowledge the failures of the past and present. The evidence that other nations have, in whole or in part, achieved these ambitions, provides an ample example that it would be entirely negligent to ignore.

The nature and extent of victims' 'rights', and thus the ability of victims to extend mercy, are pivotal issues and ones to which considerable discussion has been devoted in the foregoing chapters. These have proved to be a matter of contention in the past, but upon at least questionable grounds. They do, however, imply a need for mediation processes *within* the criminal justice structure, and are inextricably linked to decisions as to prosecution and also to sentencing. Until this situation is resolved along lines at least consistent with the suggestions advanced here, progress will be hindered by prevarication and delay.

And finally by way of conclusion, it will have become evident that in spite of the need for reform within criminal justice, retribution and restoration *via* reparation are far from mutually exclusive constructs. Criminal (and other) offending must have consequences, but these consequences must also accrue to the benefit of all the stake-holders in justice: the state, victims, offenders and communities. Contemporary criminal justice may satisfy the needs of the state, but does little to meet those of all the other legitimate stake-holders left in the wake of its processes.

A Personal Reflection

The months spent in writing this book have proved to be a journey and also a revelation. The journey was of an entirely uphill nature from a place named 'Nowhere' to another named 'Somewhere', across featureless terrain without any signposts to indicate the distance between the two. All that I knew for certain was that 'Nowhere' was a place where few people wanted to live but were somehow fearful of leaving, and that 'Somewhere' was said to be a place of promise, but its actual location was altogether uncertain. And so the journey had to be undertaken, and it transpired that while I was making it the name 'Somewhere' had been changed to 'Mercy'.

If this explanation seems to be located somewhat between John Bunyan and Lewis Carroll, I believe that it actually reflects both the reality and the uncertainty of the journey upon which I set out. The years of increasing professional dissatisfaction with explanations of criminal justice theory and practice—particularly in relation to criminal punishment—somehow compelled a search for a more enlightened avenue of approach to what is, after all, a serious and pressing social problem. This search was given impetus by an acute awareness that in Britain in particular over the past two decades criminal justice has become increasingly merciless towards offenders, while at the same time almost studiously avoiding affording victims of crime the status and empowerment that they evidently deserve.

Restorative justice has emerged and attracted increasing support worldwide as a potential means of redressing this distressing situation, though at present it sits somewhat uncomfortably alongside traditionally entrenched retributive justice due to the questions that it asks and the prescriptions that it advances for doing justice better. It is thus not a favoured form of bed-time reading for risk-averse politicians or their policy advisers. The concept of mercy however, re-defined to free it from confusion with mitigation, and developed within a restorative philosophy of justice, is I have become convinced, the missing ingredient in a more humane and purposeful form of justice delivery for the future. That is what this book has set out to propose.

Bibliography

Alexander, L and Moore, M (2007/2012Rev), 'Deontological Ethics', in *The Stanford Encyclopedia of Philosophy*, E N Zalta (ed.), (Winter 2012 edition), also available at: http://www.plato.stanford.edu/archives/win2012/entries/ethics-deontological/.

American Friends Service Committee (1972), *Struggle for Justice*, New York: Hill & Wang.

Andersen, P (2013), 'Development of Restorative Justice Processes in Norway', in D J Cornwell, J R Blad and M Wright (eds.), *Civilising Criminal Justice*, Sherfield-on-Loddon: Waterside Press, pp.479-500.

Ashworth, A (1992), 'What Victims of Crime Deserve', Paper presented to the *Fullbright Colloquium on Penal Theory and Penal Practice*, University of Stirling (September).

Ashworth, A (1993), 'Victim Impact Statements and Sentencing', *Criminal Law Review*, pp,498-509.

Barnett, R (1977), 'Restitution: A New Paradigm of Criminal Justice', *Ethics: An International Journal of Social, Political and Legal Philosophy*, 87(4), 279-301.

Bean, P (1981), *Punishment: A Philosophical Inquiry*, London: Martin Robertson and Company.

Bentham, J (1796), 'Anarchical Fallacies', in J Waldron (ed.), *Theories of Rights*, Oxford: Oxford University Press.

Blad, J R (2003), 'Against Penal Populism: Building a Global Alliance for Restorative Justice Processes and Family Empowerment', proceedings of the *4th International Conference on Conferencing, Circles and Other Restorative Practices*, Veldhoven, Netherlands, pp.130-141.

Blad, J R (2006), 'The Seductiveness of Punishment and the Case for Restorative Justice: The Netherlands', in D J Cornwell, *Criminal Punishment and Restorative Justice*, Sherfield-on-Loddon: Waterside Press, pp.135-148.

Bottoms, A E (1980), 'An Introduction to "The Coming Crisis"', in A E Bottoms and R H Preston, *The Coming Penal Crisis: A Criminological and Theological Exploration*, Edinburgh: Scottish Academic Press.

Bottoms, A E (1977), 'Reflections on the Renaissance of Dangerousness', *Howard Journal of Criminal Justice*, vol.16, pp.70-96.

Braithwaite, J (2002), *Restorative Justice and Responsive Regulation*, Oxford: Oxford University Press.

Card, C (1972), 'On Mercy', *Philosophical Review*, 81, pp.182-207.

Carter, P (2003), *Managing Offenders, Reducing Crime—A New Approach*, London: Cabinet Office Strategy Unit.

Cavadino, M and Dignan, J (1997), 'Reparation, Restitution and Rights', in *International Review of Victimology*, vol.4, pp.233-253.

Christie, N (1977), 'Conflicts as Property', *British Journal of Criminology*, 17 (1), 1-15.

Cornwell, D J (2007), *Doing Justice Better: The Politics of Restorative Justice*, Sherfield-on-Loddon: Waterside Press.

Cornwell, D J (2009), *The Penal Crisis and the Clapham Omnibus: Questions and Answers in Restorative Justice*, Sherfield-on-Loddon: Waterside Press.

Cornwell, D J (2010), 'Reparatieve en Herstelgerichte Strafrechts-Pleging: Een Goed Argument Voor Twee-Sporigheid in Strafrechtelijk Beleid? in *Tijdschrift voor Herstelrecht*, Den Haag, NL: Boom Juridische Uitgevers, pp.7-20.

Cornwell, D J (2012), 'The Need for Correctional Logic: Are Punishment and Restoration Mutually Exclusive Imperatives in Criminal Justice?' in *Nottingham Law Journal*, vol.21, pp.74-85.

Cornwell, D J (2013), 'Retribution or Restoration in Criminal Justice: Does There Have to be a Choice?—Paper to a Colloquium on Criminal Justice, Hatfield College, Durham (November).

Cullen, F T, Fisher, B S and Applegate B K (2000), 'Public Opinion About Punishment and Corrections', in M Tonry (ed.), *Crime and Justice: A Review of Research*, 27, Chicago ILL: University of Chicago Press.

Dryden, J (Date Unknown), 'The Conquest of Granada', Part1.1.i, quoted in *The Penguin Dictionary of Quotations,* Harmondsworth: Penguin Books, p.49 (1977 edition).

Duff, R A (2009a), *Justice, Mercy and Punishment*, 16 September 2009, URL: http://cjsscotland.org/index.php/cjsscotland/dynamic_ page/?id=74.

Duff, R A (2009b), *Mercy and Criminal Justice: A Response to Lindsay Farmer*, 16th November 2009, URL: http://cjscotland.org.uk/index.php/cjscotland/dynamic_page/?id=77.

Eglash, A (1977), 'Beyond Restitution: Creative Restitution', in J Hudson and B Galway (eds.), *Restitution in Criminal Justice*, Lexington, MA: D.C. Heath and Company.

Esmée Fairbairn Foundation (EFF) (2004), *Crime, Courts and Confidence: Report of an Independent Inquiry Into Alternatives to Prison*, [The Coulsfield Report], London: The Stationery Office.

Frankel, M E (1973), *Criminal Sentences*, New York: Hill & Wang.

Fogel, D (1975), *We Are the Living Proof: the Justice Model of Corrections*, Cincinnati: Anderson.

Farmer, L (2009), *Mercy and Criminal Justice: A Reply to Anthony Duff*, 16th November 2009, URL: http://bit.ly/QiMiQ

Garland, D (2002), *The Culture of Control*, Oxford: Oxford University Press.

Gavrielides, T (2011), 'Restorative Practices: From the Early Societies to the 1970s', *Internet Journal of Criminology*, www.internetjournalofcriminology.com.

Geis, G (1977), 'Restitution by Criminal Offenders: A Summary and Overview', in J Hudson and B Galway (eds.), *Restitution in Criminal Justice*, Lexington, MA: Lexington Books.

Gibson, B (2009), *The Pocket A-Z of Criminal Justice*, Sherfield-on-Loddon: Waterside Press.

Glendon, M (1991), *Rights Talk: The Impoverishment of Political Discourse*, New York: Free Press.

Grimshaw, R *et al.* (2010), *Prison and Probation Expenditure 1999-2009*, London: Centre for Crime and Justice Studies, Kings College.

Hansard, House of Commons (2010), c.155, London: House of Commons.

Hart, H L A (1961), *The Concept of Law*, Oxford: Oxford University Press.

Hart, H L A (1982), *Essays on Bentham: Studies in Jurisprudence and Political Theory*, Oxford: Clarendon Press.

Hestevold, H S (1985), 'Justice to Mercy', *Philosophy and Phenomenological Research*, vol.46, no.2.

Hohfeld, W (1919), *Fundamental Logical Conceptions*, W Cook (ed.), New Haven: Yale University Press.

Holdsworth, S W (1956), *A History of English Law*, London: Methuen.

Holmes, S and Sunstein, S (1999), *The Costs of Rights*, New York: W W Norton.

Home Office (1964), *The Prison Rules*, SI 388, London: HMSO.

Home Office (1990), *Victim's Charter: A Statement of Rights of Victims*, London: HMSO.

Home Office (1996), *Victim's Charter: A Statement of Standards for Victims of Crime*, London: HMSO.

Home Office (2001a), *Making Punishments Work*, [The Halliday Report], London: Home Office.

Home Office (2001b), *A Review of the Victim's Charter*, London: Home Office Communications Directorate.

Home Office (2003a), *Restorative Justice: The Government's Strategy*, [Consultation Document], London: Home Office Communications Directorate.

Home Office (2003b), *A New Deal for Victims and Witnesses: National Strategy to Deliver Improved Services*, London: Home Office.

Home Office (2005a), *Victims' Rights'*, London: Home Office.

Home Office (2005b), *The Code of Practice for Victims of Crime*, London: HMSO (October).

Home Office (2005c), *Re-building Lives—Supporting Victims of Crime*, CM 6705, London: HMSO (December).

Home Office (2005d), *Government Proposes New Compensation Arrangements and Better Support for Victims of Crime*, at: http://www.cjp.org.uk/news/archive/government-proposes-new-compensation-arrangements-and-better-support-for-victims-of-crime-07-12-2005/ of 7 December.

Home Office (2011), *Home Office Statistical Bulletin (20 April)*, at: www.statistics.gov.uk.

Honderich, T (1971), *Punishment: The Supposed Justifications*, Harmondsworth: Penguin Books.

House of Commons Library (2013), *Prison Population Statistics*, [Authors: G Bermand and A Dar], SN/SG/4344, London: House of Commons (29 July).

Hudson, B (1987), *Justice Through Punishment*, Basingstoke: Macmillan Education.

International Centre for Prison Studies (2012), *World Prison Brief*, at: http://www.prisonstudies.org/info/worldbrief/

Jackson, R M (1940), *Machinery of Justice in England*, J R Spencer (ed.), Cambridge: Cambridge University Press.

Jeudwine, J (1917), *Tort, Crime and Police in Medieval Britain*, London: Williams and Norgate.

Joutsen, M, Rahti, R and Pölönen, P (2001), *Criminal Justice Systems in Europe and North America — Finland*, Helsinki: Academic Bookstore.

Kleinig, J (1978), 'Crime and the Concept of Harm', *American Philosophical Quarterly*, 15, pp.27-36.

Kramer, M (2001), 'Getting Rights Right', in J Kramer (ed.), *Rights, Wrongs and Responsibilities*, London: Macmillan, pp.28-95.

Kramer, M, Simmonds, M and Steiner, H (1998), *A Debate Over Rights*, Oxford: Oxford University Press.

Kyvsgaard, B (2001), 'Penal Sanctions and the Use of Imprisonment in Denmark', in M Tonry (ed.), *Penal Reform in Overcrowded Times*, New York: Oxford University Press.

Lappi-Seppälä, T (2001), 'Sentencing and Punishment in Finland: The Decline of the Repressive Ideal', in M Tonry and R S Frase (eds.), *Punishment and Penal Systems in Western Countries*, New York: Oxford University Press, pp.92-150.

Lappi-Seppälä, T (2013), 'Downsizing the Use of Imprisonment in Finland', in D J Cornwell, J R Blad and M Wright (eds.), *Civilising Criminal Justice*, Sherfield-on-Loddon: Waterside Press, 501-524.

Larsson, P. (2001), 'Norway Prison Use Up Slightly: Community Penalty Lots', in M Tonry (ed.), *Penal Reform in Overcrowded Times*, New York: Oxford University Press.

Lauchs, M (2005), 'Justice and Equity v. Mercy', *Australian Association for Professional and Applied Ethics 12th Annual Conference*, Adelaide, (28-30 September).

Lewis, W W (1987), *The Governance of Norman and Angevin England 1086-1272*, Stanford, ILL: Stanford University Press.

Lord Chief Justice of England (2001), *Practice Direction (Crime: Victim Personal Statements)*, 4 All ER 640: III. 28.

Lyons, D (1970), 'The Correlativity of Rights and Duties', in *Nous*, 4, pp.45-57.

Lyons, D (1994), *Rights, Welfare and Mill's Moral Theory*, Oxford: Oxford University Press.

Maruna, S and King, A (2004), 'Public Opinion and Community Penalties', in A E Bottoms, S Rex and G Robinson (eds.), *Alternatives to Prison: Options for an Insecure Society*, Collompton: Willan Publishing.

Mbambo, B And Skelton, A (2003), 'Preparing the South African Community for Implementing a New Child Justice System', in L Walgrave (ed.), *Repositioning Restorative Justice*, Cullompton, Devon,UK: Willan Publishing, pp.271-283.

Ministry of Justice (2007), *Securing the Future: Proposals for the Sustainable Use of Custody in England and Wales*, [Report by Lord Carter of Coles], London: Ministry of Justice.

Ministry of Justice (2010), *Compendium of Reoffending Statistics*, London: Ministry of Justice.

Ministry of Justice (2012a), *Restorative Justice Action Plan for the Criminal Justice System*, London: Ministry of Justice.

Ministry of Justice (2012b), *Facing up to Offending: Restorative Justice in the Criminal Justice System*, [Report of the Criminal Justice Joint Inspectorate], London: Ministry of Justice.

Ministry of Justice (2012c), *Monthly Population Bulletin April 2012*, London: Ministry of Justice.

Ministry of Justice (2012d), *Criminal Justice Statistics Quarterly Update to December 2011* [Table Q5.1], London: Ministry of Justice.

Ministry of Justice (2012e), 'Cost per Place and Cost per Prisoner by Individual Prison' [Table 1], *National Offender Management Service Annual Report and Accounts 2010-2011—Management Information Addendum*, London: Ministry of Justice.

Ministry of Justice (2012f), *Getting it Right for Victims and Witnesses*, Consultation Paper CP3/2012, CM 8288, London: Ministry of Justice.

Ministry of Justice (2012g), *Proven Re-offending Quarterly—January to December 2010*, London: Ministry of Justice.

More, T S [1990] (1515), *Utopia: New Haven*, London: Yale University Press.

Morgan, P (1978), *Delinquent Fantasies*, London: Temple Smith.

Morris, A (1978), *Juvenile Justice*, London: Heinemann.

Morris, N. (1974), *The Future of Imprisonment*, Chicago, ILL: University of Chicago Press.

Murphy, J G (1986), 'Mercy and Legal Justice', *Social Philosophy and Policy*, 4, reprinted in J G Murphy and J Hampton (1988), *Forgiveness and Mercy*, Cambridge: Cambridge University Press.

Narveson, J (2001), *The Libertarian Idea*, Peterborough, Ontario: Broadview.

National Audit Office (2010), *Managing Offenders on Short Custodial Sentences*, London: NAO.

Nussbaum, M (1993), 'Equity and Mercy', *Philosophy and Public Affairs*, vol.22, pp.94-5.

Office for National Statistics (2011), *Crime in England and Wales Quarterly Update to December 2010*, London: ONS.

O'Niell, O (1996), *Toward Justice and Virtue: A Constructive Account of Practical Reasoning*, Cambridge: Cambridge University Press.

Pollock, F and Maitland, F W (1898), *The History of English Criminal Law before the Time of Edward I*, Cambridge: Cambridge University Press.

Prison Reform Trust (2012a), *Bromley Briefings Prison Factfile*, London: Prison Reform Trust (June).

Prison Reform Trust (2012b), *Bromley Briefings Prison Factfile*, London: Prison Reform Trust (November).

Rainbolt, G W (1990), 'Mercy: An Independent, Imperfect Virtue', *American Philosophy Quarterly*, vol.27, no.2, pp.169-173.

Restorative Justice Council (2011), *What Does the Ministry of Justice RJ Research Tell Us?*. London:RJC, at http://www.restorativejustice.org.uk/news/what_does_the_ministry_of_justice_research_into_restorative_justice_tell_us/

Roberts, J V and Stalans, L (eds.) (1997), *Public Opinion, Crime and Criminal Justice*, Boulder, COL: Westview Press.

Roberts, J V, Stalans, L, Indermauer, D and Hough, M (eds.) (2003), *Penal Populism and Public Opinion: Lessons From Five Countries*, Oxford and New York: Oxford University Press.

Robinson, P (2012), 'Mercy, Crime Control and Moral Credibility', in A Sarat (ed.). *Merciful Judgements and Contemporary Society: Legal Problems, Legal Possibilities*, Cambridge: Cambridge University Press.

Sadler, G (2006), 'Mercy and Justice in Saint Anselm's Prologion', A*merican Catholic Philosophical Quarterly*, Vol.80, No.1, pp.41-61.

Schur, E (1973), *Radical Nonintervention: Rethinking the Delinquency Problem*, Englewood Cliffs, NJ: Prentice-Hall.

Seneca, L A (*circa* 30AD), 'On Mercy', *Moral Essays,*II.ii.2.iv [Tr. J.W. Basore], The Loeb Classical Library, London: Heinemann.

Shapland, J, Atkinson, A, Atkinson, H, Chapman, B, Dignan, J, Howes, M, Johnstone, J, Robinson, G and Sorsby, A (2007), *Restorative Justice: The Views of Victims and Offenders*, Third Report, Centre for Criminological Research, University of Sheffield and Ministry of Justice, London: Ministry of Justice.

Sharpe, S (2004), 'How Large Should the Restorative Justice "Tent" Be?' in H Zehr and B Toews (eds.), *Critical Issues in Restorative Justice*, Cullompton, : Willan Publishing, pp.17-31.

Smart, A (1968), 'Mercy', *Philosophy*, vol.43, pp.345-359. Also reprinted in H B Acton (ed.) (1969), *The Philosophy of Punishment: A Collection of Papers*, London: Macmillan, pp.212-228.

Stackpole, R (Undated), 'Saint Thomas Aquinas on the Virtue of Mercy'. Commentary at: http://thedivinemercy.org/library/article.php

Steiner, H (1994), *An Essay on Rights*, Oxford: Blackwell.

Tak, P (2001), 'Sentencing and Punishment in The Netherlands', in M Tonry and R S Frase (eds.), *Sentencing and Sanctions in Western Countries*, New York: Oxford University Press.

Tasioulas, J (2003), 'Mercy', *Proceedings of the Aristotelian Society*, vol.103, no.2, pp.101-132.

Thomson, J (1990), *The Realm of Rights*, Cambridge: Harvard University Press.

Tonry, M (ed.) (2003), *Confronting Crime: Crime Control Policy Under New Labour*, Cullompton: Willan Publishing.

Twambly, P (1985), 'Mercy and Forgiveness', *Analysis*, vol.36, pp.84-90.

Tutu, D M (Abp) (1999), *No Future Without Forgiveness*, London: Rider Publishing and New York: Doubleday.

Umbreit, M S, Vos, B, Coates, R B and Lightfoot, E (2005), 'Restorative Justice in the Twenty-First Century: A Social Movement Full of Opportunities and Pitfalls', *Marquette Law Review*, vol.89, no.2, 251-304.

Von Hirsch, A (1976), *Doing Justice*, New York: Hill & Wang).

Von Hirsch, A (1985), *Past of Future Crimes: Deservedness and Dangerousness in the Sentencing of Criminals*, Manchester: Manchester University Press.

Walker, P N (1972), *Punishment: An Illustrated History*, Newton Abbot: David and Charles (Publishers) Limited.

Wellman, C (1985), *A Theory of Rights*, Totowa, NJ: Rowman and Allanheld.

Wenar, L (2011), 'Rights', in *Stanford Encyclopedia of Philosophy*, E N Zalta (ed.), available at: http://plato.stanford.edu/entries/rights/

Wiegend, T (2001), 'Sentencing and Punishment in Germany', in M Tonry and R S Frase (eds.), *Sentencing and Sanctions in Western Countries*, New York: Oxford University Press.

Wilkins, L (1980), 'Sentencing Guidelines to Reduce Disparity', *Criminal Law Review*, April, 201-4.

Wilson, J (1977), *Thinking About Crime*, New York: Vintage Press.

Wright, M (1996), 'Can Mediation be an Alternative to Criminal Justice', in B Galway and J Hudson (eds.), *Restorative Justice: International Perspectives*, Monsey, NY: Criminal Justice Press.

Zehr, H (1990), *Changing Lenses: A New Focus for Crime and Justice*, Scottdale, PA: Herald Press.

Zehr, H (2002), *The Little Book of Restorative Justice*, Intercourse, PA: Good Books.

Zehr, H and Mika, H (1998), 'Fundamental Concepts of Restorative Justice', *Contemporary Justice Review*, 1(1), 47-55.

Zehr, H and Toews, B (eds.) (2004), *Critical Issues in Restorative Justice*, Cullompton: Willan Publishing.

Index

R

S

T

U

V

Criminal Punishment and Restorative Justice: Past, Present and Future Perspectives

by David J Cornwell. With a Foreword by Tony Cameron

'Well worth the time and effort to read and ponder, especially for anyone who actually works in or administers 'punishment' within criminal justice programmes': restorativejustice.org

Paperback & ebook | ISBN 978-1-904380-20-7 | 2006 | 186 pages

Doing Justice Better: The Politics of Restorative Justice

by David J Cornwell. With a Foreword by Mark S Umbreit

'This book identifies the organizational stresses and strains, the target-setting, the policy "blips" and all the problems of trying to bring radical change to our criminal justice system': Sir Charles Pollard QPM

Paperback & ebook | ISBN 978-1-904380-34-4 | 2007 | 200 pages

The Penal Crisis and the Clapham Omnibus: Questions and Answers in Restorative Justice

by David J Cornwell. With a Foreword by Heather Strang

'A welcome contribution to criminal justice debate. Many books have championed the virtues of restorative justice; *The Penal Crisis* tackles the altogether more difficult dimension of [how] to articulate how restorative justice might be achieved in practice': *Howard League Journal*

Paperback & ebook | ISBN 978-1-904380-47-4 | 2009 | 256 pages

Lightning Source UK Ltd.
Milton Keynes UK
UKOW04f0339080714

234748UK00001B/9/P